BUSES

YEARBOOK 2018

Edited by STEWART J. BROWN

BUSES

YEARBOOK 2018

FRONT COVER: *Leicester's modern bus fleet includes this Arriva ADL Enviro400 MMC.* Stewart J Brown

BACK COVER (UPPER): *One of London's distinctive New Routemasters heads for Hammersmith.* David Jukes

BACK COVER (LOWER): *The Optare Versa has been around for ten years. This striking Starship is in Burnley.* Mark Bailey

PREVIOUS PAGE: *Scottish variety with, from the left, a Bristol RE, a Seddon Pennine and a Bristol Lodekka in Edinburgh, all operated by Eastern Scottish.* Peter Rowlands

THIS PAGE: *The Optare Versa is popular with many small fleets. This bus is in the fleet of Fife company Moffat & Williamson.* Mark Bailey

Published by Key Publishing Ltd.
www.keypublishing.com

First Published July 2017

ISBN: 978-1-910415-32-0

Printed in England by
Gomer Press Ltd
Llandysul Enterprise Park
Llandysul
Ceredigion
SA44 4JL

www.busesmag.com

A year of great change
Alan Millar...3

New Routemaster variety...
Richard Walter..................................17

Bournemouth's yellow buses
Michael H C Baker............................24

Shuttle Success
Billy Nicol...30

Out of Africa
Stewart J Brown..............................36

Happy Anniversary
Mark Bailey......................................44

Twenty years of D&G
Cliff Beeton......................................52

Isle of Man – a return visit
John Young.......................................62

Regrets? I've had a few
Gavin Booth......................................65

Ipswich Buses, a local authority survivor
Geoff Mills..72

Bradford Corporation's London RTs
Stuart Emmett...................................80

Looks familiar?
Sholto Thomas..................................85

Five years on the Hammersmith Road
David Jukes.......................................90

Snapshot Leicester
Stewart J Brown..............................100

Going their own way
Peter Rowlands...............................103

Merseyside memories
John Robinson.................................112

Bus blues
Robert E Jowitt...............................121

Transport Act 1968

CHAPTER 73

ARRANGEMENT OF SECTIONS

PART I

INTEGRATION OF FREIGHT TRANSPORT SERVICES

The National Freight Corporation

Section
1. Establishment and general duty of Freight Corporation.
2. General powers of Freight Corporation.
3. Financial provisions with respect to Freight Corporation.

Transfer of assets, etc.

4. Transfer to Freight Corporation of certain securities, rights and liabilities.
5. Formation by Railways Board of, and transfer to Freight Corporation of shares in, subsidiary companies.

The Freight Integration Council

6. The Freight Integration Council.

Redistribution of activities between Freight Corporation and Railways Board or Scottish Group

7. Transfer schemes by authorities.
8. Transfer orders by Minister.

PART II

PASSENGER TRANSPORT AREAS

Designation of Passenger Transport Areas and establishment and functions of Authorities and Executives

9. Passenger Transport Areas, Authorities and Executives.
10. General powers of Executive.
11. Financial duty of Executive.
12. Borrowing powers of Executive.
13. Power for Authority to precept for Executive.
14. Accounts of Executive.
15. Further functions of Authority.
16. Publication of annual report by Authority and Executive and prevention of improper conduct of subsidiary activities.

A

Reorganisation of passenger transport in Passenger Transport Areas

Section
17. Transfer to Executive of local authority transport undertakings.
18. Planning of passenger transport services in designated areas.
19. Transfer of control of bus services to Executive.
20. Special duty of certain Executives with respect to railway passenger services.
21. Provisions as to functions of traffic commissioners in connection with designated areas.

General

22. Provisions as to regulations and orders under Part II.
23. Consents of, or directions by, Minister under Part II.

PART III

BUS AND FERRY SERVICES

National Bus Company and Scottish Transport Group

24. Establishment and general duties of Bus Company and Scottish Group.
25. General powers of Bus Company.
26. General powers of Scottish Group.
27. Financial provisions with respect to Bus Company and Scottish Group.
28. Transfer to Bus Company or Scottish Group of certain securities, rights and liabilities.
29. Transfer of certain property, rights and liabilities between Railways Board and Bus Company or Scottish Group.

Relaxation of control over certain bus services

30. Permit for certain bus services in lieu of road service licence.
31. Abolition of special control over bus services provided by local authorities outside their areas.

Assistance for bus and ferry services

32. New bus grants.
33. Grants towards duty charged on bus fuel.
34. Assistance for rural bus or ferry services.

A year of great change

Fifty years on, *Buses* editor **Alan Millar** considers the impact of the Transport Act 1968 and the creation of the British Leyland Motor Corporation.

Half a century ago, Britain's bus industry was turned upside down by a landmark piece of legislation. Politicians sunk their teeth into such things at roughly 20-year intervals, with the 1930 Road Traffic Act and the Transport Acts of 1947, 1968 and 1985 all ushering in huge change to the structure of the industry and provision of bus services.

They went for the double in 1968, for besides the new Transport Act, the government of the day also brokered a motor industry merger that created British Leyland. By the end of the year, they had helped concentrate the supply and purchase of buses in far fewer, but much larger hands.

Like the Acts of 1930 and 1947, the legislation of 1968 was the work of a Labour government.

This was Harold Wilson's administration elected in 1964 with a wafer-thin majority and re-elected two years later with a comfortable 96 seats over the combined opposition. An administration whose determination to do something about public transport began with the appointment in December 1965 of Barbara Castle, one of the most effective of its performers, as minister of transport.

She had been an MP since 1945 and picked up where her predecessors had left off when defeated in 1951. That government had brought substantial parts of the bus industry into state ownership and was on the brink of setting up the first of a suite of regional transport boards — miniature London Transports if you will — with compulsory powers to acquire most other

ABOVE: *Tyneside was one of the first four conurbations in which a PTE — the organisations first conceived as Conurbation Transport Authorities — were to deliver integrated public transport. It retained the yellow and cream livery of Newcastle Corporation, to whom this Alexander-bodied Leyland Atlantean was new in 1968.*

operators and provide an integrated service of buses and trains that eliminated the perceived waste of overlapping or competing routes.

Fourteen years on, Castle was charged once again with delivering her party's cherished dream of an integrated transport system and the 1968 Act was meant to achieve it. The bigger parts of the bus industry not yet in public ownership were to be brought into state ownership and the regional board idea was revived with conurbation transport authorities (CTAs), starting in four city regions.

The 14 years since 1951 had seen a huge reverse in the fortunes of Britain's public transport. Car ownership was rising rapidly, and with it came demands to accommodate cars on an expanded road network when they were moving, in urban car parks when they reached their destinations, and for car-owning Britons to be housed in low density homes with gardens and somewhere to park their cars.

Demand for bus travel was in consequent free-fall, made worse by the parallel social change that saw television replace cinema for much entertainment and also by the car-generated traffic congestion that made bus travel seem an inferior means of getting from A to B. The railways

also were contracting on an unprecedented scale, as Dr Richard Beeching began closing around a quarter of the network in a plan unveiled in 1963.

The object of the 1968 Act — the Utopian dream of those who inspired it — was to create a superior public transport service that offered a quality alternative to the car. A service for the rest of the country that matched what London Transport had aspired to deliver in its first and only five-year plan of 1935-40, with buses and Underground trains meeting at elegantly designed interchange stations.

The Act was about far more than public transport and one of the paradoxes of those times is that at the same time as it tightened public control of buses, the government effectively deregulated road freight haulage along lines that a later Conservative government would adopt for buses and coaches in the 1980s.

NBC and STG

The expansion of public ownership was to be achieved by creating a National Bus Company (NBC), bringing into state ownership the greater part of the industry still partly or wholly in private sector control.

Nationalisation of the railways in 1948 had

brought with it their shareholdings in regional bus companies, prompting two of the three groups that owned most of them — Thomas Tilling and Scottish Motor Traction — to sell their remaining shareholdings (generally 50 per cent) to the state, which continued to run them as commercial companies that happened now to be in public ownership.

The third of these groups, British Electric Traction, held out against public ownership and when it felt threatened it quite vociferously opposed the very idea, even though most of its companies also were part owned by the state. Its companies served urban and rural areas across northern and south-eastern England, the Midlands and South Wales.

Completely private enterprises, usually in family ownership, were steadily disappearing. The events of 1948 prompted several larger ones to sell up voluntarily, perhaps suspecting that the financial recompense of compulsory purchases would be a lot less generous. And as they got older and wanted to retire, and the decline in bus use worsened from the late 1950s, many owners of small to medium independents also sold out, either to the state-owned businesses or BET.

From 1962, state ownership of buses outside London (and some other business interests including road haulage) was held by the Transport Holding Company (THC), which controlled the former Tilling companies in England and Wales along with businesses acquired since 1948, and the similarly expanded former SMT group which was managed collectively as the Scottish Bus Group (SBG).

By one means or another, NBC was to acquire the BET companies but — possibly in response to fresh stirrings of Scottish nationalism — THC's buses north of the border would go to a new Edinburgh-controlled Scottish Transport Group (STG), along with essential west coast shipping services.

The Scottish restructure reflected something unchanged in 50 years: that some other forms of public transport excite public and politicians far more than buses. In much of Britain in 2017/18 it is trains. In Scotland half a century ago — and today — it also is shipping services on lifeline routes to islands and remote parts of the mainland.

Those operated on the Clyde and to the Isle of Skye were already in state ownership, provided by the Caledonian Steam Packet Company, a British Rail subsidiary. The rest belonged to

ABOVE: *Most of the buses in THC's former Tilling fleets had Bristol chassis and ECW bodies, like this Lodekka LD6G operating for Crosville in Llandudno in 1970. Both manufacturers were wholly owned by THC until 1965.*

David MacBrayne, which like BET's buses were part owned by the state and part by the private sector, in this case the Coast Lines shipping company, which in 1971 became part of P&O.

The Scottish civil service had been wrestling for some time with what to do about MacBrayne, which provided essential but unprofitable services, and in 1964 an investment in its first sea-going vehicle ferries was achieved by placing them in government ownership for MacBrayne to operate as its own.

Lumping buses and ships together — MacBrayne and Caledonian Steam Packet — from the beginning of 1969 (and buying out the Coast Lines shareholding) seemed like an accountant's and politician's perfect solution — using SBG's healthy profits to cross-subsidise the ships. The shipping operation was merged later into a single company, Caledonian MacBrayne, and MacBrayne's buses were either absorbed into SBG or sold to local operators.

It took until late October 1968 for the Act to receive the Royal Assent and pass into law, but by then the missing piece in the NBC jigsaw was well in place. To the outside world, BET projected a message of defiance against public ownership, with buses carrying advertising denouncing the government's plans, but it was quietly bowing to the inevitable and sought a sale on the best terms available.

A deal announced in November 1967 saw THC buy its British bus interests — around 11,000 vehicles — for £35million; that is nearly £600million in today's money. Shortly beforehand, one of the largest independent operators, the 450-vehicle West Riding Automobile Company, accepted a £1.9million bid from THC.

While the jigsaw was in place, NBC did not come into formal existence until the first day of 1969, when it also acquired some railway-owned buses in four municipal fleets in Yorkshire. It grew substantially one year later when the government transferred London Transport from state to local authority control, but kept its country buses and Green Line coaches, placing them in NBC's newly created London Country Bus Services subsidiary and taking its fleet strength up to 22,000.

More growth came in 1970 with the acquisitions of the Gosport & Fareham Omnibus Company's Provincial business, Venture Transport in County Durham and the municipal undertakings in Exeter and Luton. Perhaps there might have been more, but Labour unexpectedly lost the 1970 general election and some of the impetus behind NBC was gone.

To begin with, NBC was unknown to the travelling public. It was the invisible parent company behind around 60 regional trading names. It changed some of those names, notably where BET had retained small subsidiaries that NBC merged into larger neighbours. Some of its restructures were more ambitious, like merging Thames Valley and Aldershot & District to form Alder Valley — a fabricated name unknown to students of geography.

NBC started making its name known from 1972 when it adopted a corporate livery style for its buses and coaches, and backed this up with advertising campaigns designed to make the public believe in its greatness.

The birth of the PTEs

While the Transport Bill that became the 1968 Act was being debated in parliament, Barbara Castle gave the impression that NBC might only be a transient being. Her favoured vehicle for change — the means of delivering the Holy Grail of integration — were the CTAs.

There was some question about whether these would operate public transport services or simply oversee their provision. The latter was the way things were — and still are — done in Germany, but a visit to the United States in 1966 sold her the apparent benefits of the way that public transport investment was being delivered in conurbations like San Francisco and Boston.

Fifteen years earlier, some of the strongest objections to the stillborn area transport boards came from councils — many of them Labour controlled — who relished not one jot the prospect of their bus undertakings being taken away. They were little more enthusiastic in 1967/68, especially in the smaller towns whose buses were destined to be hoovered up by a larger neighbour, but such objections were either ignored or mitigated as the plans passed into law.

And so it was that between October 1969 and January 1970 the operations of 20 municipalities were bundled into four PTEs. West Midlands combined the huge Birmingham undertaking — the largest municipal fleet in Britain — with the Black Country undertakings in Walsall, Wolverhampton and West Bromwich. Merseyside combined Liverpool with the Wirral undertakings of Birkenhead and Wallasey, while Tyneside took ownership of the Newcastle and South Shields operations that were separated by the River Tyne and a substantial mileage between their respective outer termini.

The biggest act of amalgamation was at Selnec,

ABOVE: *STG transferred most of MacBrayne's bus services to Scottish Bus Group subsidiaries in 1970/71. Highland Omnibuses took over the majority of them, including this Duple-bodied Bedford C5Z1 in its grey and blue coach livery at Tarbert, Harris in the Outer Hebrides.*

where Manchester and 10 other undertakings (the smallest was Ramsbottom with just 14 buses) came together as one. While the other three preserved at least a semblance of identity of the largest of their constituent fleets (Merseyside had a separate livery for its Wirral operation), Selnec threw all tradition to the wind and embraced its bold new future with a modern — if perhaps impractical — livery of sunglow orange and white.

A fourth PTE followed for Greater Glasgow in 1973 (Glasgow's was the only municipal undertaking available for it to acquire), while local government reorganisation brought two more for West and South Yorkshire in 1974. At the same time Selnec became Greater Manchester and absorbed Wigan, Merseyside absorbed Southport and St Helens, West Midlands was enlarged to take in Coventry, and Tyneside became Tyne & Wear and took in Sunderland.

For a time, it looked like the dismemberment of NBC could really happen. The PTEs were charged with delivering integrated public transport and had powers to reach agreements with British Rail and other bus operators to provide services on their behalf.

The railway bit was quite easy. Already heavily subsidised, the financial support would be channeled through the local authorities funding the PTAs and PTEs rather than the state. It was trickier with buses, as NBC and SBG were still structured as commercial companies charged with remaining solvent and paying off a capital debt. The loss of profitable routes in the big city regions could undermine their ability to maintain those in other parts of the country where the profits were thinner or non-existent.

NBC agreed to sell two substantial operations to PTEs. In January 1972, most of North Western Road Car passed to Selnec and in December 1973

ABOVE: *One of NBC's first acts of reorganisation, in January 1969, was to transfer United Auto's Carlisle area services to former BET subsidiary Ribble. Twenty-one ECW-bodied Bristol single-deckers changed hands, including this 1962 MW6G.*

West Midlands took over the Midland Red business within the new West Midlands Metropolitan County. The Midland Red deal would have huge financial ramifications for the future, depriving NBC of so much profitable revenue that in 1983 it broke Midland Red into smaller companies.

NBC refused to sell out elsewhere, but reached agreements with PTEs that saw it run many services on an agency basis. In Tyne & Wear and West Yorkshire, many of its buses ran in PTE colours; in Merseyside, they displayed PTE logos.

In Greater Glasgow, PTE and SBG failed to agree on almost anything. SBG had much to lose from selling that huge part of its business to a rival public body, and in a city where too many buses were chasing declining numbers of passengers, the PTE also risked losing much in any rationalised route network. The seeds of an almighty battle for territory were being sown; one that was fought when bus services were deregulated in 1986, but that is another story for another day.

External subsidies

The 1968 Act also introduced the bus industry to external funding. Until then, the big operators maintained unremunerative services — including replacements for railways closed by Dr Beeching — by cross-subsidising them from the profitable ones. In hopelessly unprofitable places like much of Cornwall and the Scottish Highlands, they were the buyers of only resort when private operators gave up routes that were socially essential.

But with business declining everywhere, the days of cross-subsidy — at least on such a universal scale — were coming to an end and the government included in the 1968 Act the power for local authorities to subsidise the manifestly unprofitable.

It took NBC until 1970 to start seeking council support for rural services and SBG followed soon after. Once they got stuck into the process, councils found themselves faced with what amounted to an ultimatum to come up with the funds or large numbers of services would be lost.

Crosville, with an operating territory taking in large rural areas across Cheshire, Shropshire, North and Mid Wales, was one of the first to break cover, producing a long list of routes that it was no longer prepared to maintain on its own. Western National had a similarly stark proposition to put to the decision makers of Cornwall. In Scotland, Western SMT hung an axe over much of what was soon to become Dumfries & Galloway.

Many routes were lost in Cornwall while more support was found in some other parts, but this was the beginning of a steadily changing relationship between the big bus operators and the councils of the counties they served, who began exerting more control over the services they were now being asked to support.

It was a process that by the end of the 1970s had led NBC to learn far more about the service networks its companies provided, developing initiatives like its Market Analysis Project to tailor those networks to demand and to the money that was available for public subsidy.

It also was a process that helped persuade a later Conservative government to drive down the subsidy bill by exposing the supported part of the bus network to competitive tender.

New Bus Grant

The other form of internal funding to come with the Act — with major ramifications for the future — was the introduction of New Bus Grant, by which the government picked up 25 per cent of the cost of new vehicles that met its strict standards.

The essential standard was that they should be suitable for what then was called one-man operation. By removing conductors and passing fare collection on to drivers, the industry believed it could reduce its labour costs and address a problem of staff shortages that had been causing difficulties for at least 20 years.

To do this quickly, it needed more buses that could be one-man operated. Double-deckers without a conductor had only been legalised in 1966 and although many operators were buying rear-engined double-deckers that were either equipped for one-man operation or could easily be converted, some had clung to the older front-engined half-cab designs for as long as they could. London Transport's last Routemasters arrived early in 1968 and other adherents included Blackpool and Northampton Corporations, East Kent and THC's ex-Tilling companies.

A 25 per cent government contribution was either an acknowledgment that one-man designs were more expensive than their predecessors or that operators needed to accelerate their fleet replacement to phase out conductors earlier than planned. If we assume it was for the latter reason, then the grant would reduce the typical 15-year life of a conductor-operated bus to 12 years and the industry could be conductor-free by 1980.

As first implemented, the grant was to run only run for seven years, for vehicles ordered between July 1968 and August 1975. This would kick-start the process and normal purchasing arrangements

ABOVE: *This Leyland Atlantean in the Trent fleet, with Weymann lowbridge body, retained its BET era red and a cream livery in August 1973, but NBC corporate image was apparent on the advertisement on its side for Trent's travel agency.*

ABOVE: *Orange and white Selnec livery on a Daimler CVG6 with Metro-Cammell body new to Manchester Corporation in 1954. Selnec divided its operations into Central, Southern and Northern companies.*

could resume from September 1975. Most buses already on order on 8 July 1968 also qualified if they complied with most of the required standards.

The original qualification criteria were drawn extremely tightly, down to exact dimensions for wheelbase, front and rear overhang, door widths and floor height. High-floor single-deckers could be 9m, 10m or 11m, low-frame rear-engined single-deckers (known then as low-floor) could be 10m or 11m with either a stepped or ramped floor and either a horizontal or transverse vertical engine. Double-deckers could be 9.5m or 10m, either 13ft 8in or 14ft 6in high and have a transverse rear engine. Grant could be claimed in special circumstances for other vehicles, such as shorter single-deckers for routes that required them.

The standards were built around manufacturers' existing models, but also betrayed the preferences of the operators who helped influence the Ministry of Transport in drawing up the rules.

This was especially apparent with lowheight double-deckers. These could only be 9.5m long and there was no provision for a second door. The hand of the future NBC could be detected here,

as that was the only size and layout of lowheight double-deckers that the THC companies had ordered with the introduction of the new Bristol VRT.

SBG, however, had seen potential for 10m lowheight double-deckers and ordered 32 with 83 seats — seven Daimler Fleetlines and 25 of the first production VRTs — before the bus grant criteria put a stop to any more.

Some take the view that bus grant also put paid to the offside in-line engine layout of the two prototype VRs built in 1966, which were 10m lowheight double-deckers, but the timeline of events suggests that THC's initial experience with this design killed it off beforehand and that it was as far off the influential operators' shopping list as SBG's 83-seaters were when the grant criteria were drawn up.

The VRT was announced as early as June 1967 in response to the THC companies' expressed preference for a 9.5m maximum length that could only be accommodated with a transverse engine.

Another myth is that bus grant alone killed off the old half-cab designs. While it certainly accelerated their demise, they were well on their way out, with orders declining towards uneconomic numbers. The last of them, the Daimler CVG6, survived as an export model only until 1972 when Kowloon Motor Bus in Hong Kong stopped buying it.

The bus grant scheme was only three years old in 1971 when Edward Heath's Conservative government greatly extended its scope and scale. The industry had argued that it would take more than seven years to achieve the scheme's objectives and that a seven-year scheme would squeeze too many bus purchases into too short a period, causing undesirable peaks and troughs in orders.

The grant was extended to 1980, doubled to 50 per cent and some rules were relaxed. Two-door lowheight double-deckers were built for fleets that wanted them and the grant coach was created — a coach with wider doors, front destination displays and a cab suited for fare collection; provided they clocked up at least half of their mileage on stage carriage services, such coaches could be purchased effectively at half price.

While the grant was conceived as a means of accelerating the introduction of one-man operation,

it turned into a more general subsidy. There was no requirement for grant-funded buses to be operated without a conductor and although many were, large numbers in at least their earlier years had a crew of two; notably London Transport's 164 Scania/MCW Metropolitans and its large DM sub-class of Leyland Fleetlines. Some independent operators had not the slightest intention of giving up on conductor operation but could still buy new grant-funded buses.

Most of the single-deckers that grant-funded vehicles replaced were capable of conversion to one-man operation if they were not already so equipped, and by 1980 most new double-deckers were replacing vehicles with rear engines and front entrances.

Bus grant also altered some of the economics of vehicle ownership in an age when the testing regime demanded heavy overhauls to obtain new certificates of fitness after seven and 12 years. A new bus at 50 per cent of the list price could be more cost effective than the expense of overhauling a 12-year-old one

ABOVE: *Merseyside PTE took over the municipal buses of Birkenhead in December 1969 along with those of Wallasey and Liverpool, but there was little visible evidence of the change the following July. A 1954 Weymann-bodied Leyland Titan PD2/12 is in full blue and cream livery with Birkenhead Transport fleetnames and coat of arms, as are the newer Northern Counties-bodied Daimler Fleetlines behind.*

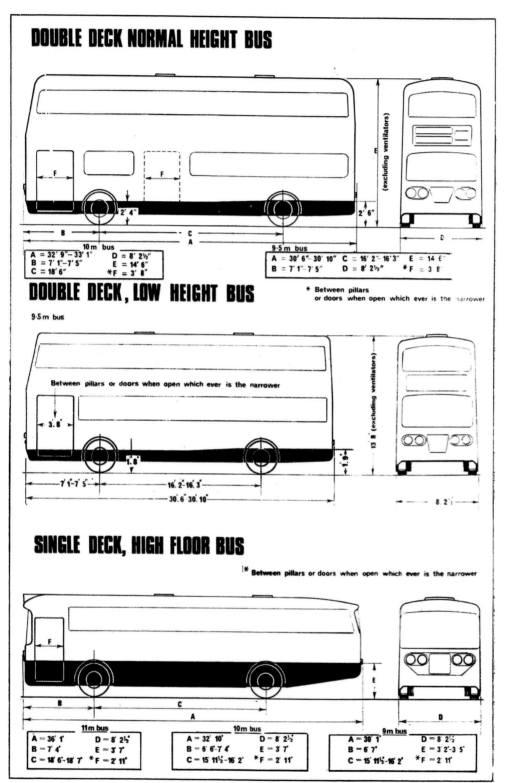

DOUBLE DECK NORMAL HEIGHT BUS

2' 4"

2' 6"

10 m bus

A = 32' 9"–33' 1"	D = 8' 2½"
B = 7' 1"–7' 5"	E = 14' 6"
C = 18' 6"	*F = 3' 8"

9·5 m bus

A = 30' 6"–30' 10"	C = 16' 2"–16' 3"	E = 14' 6"
B = 7' 1"–7' 5"	D = 8' 2½"	*F = 3 8"

E (excluding ventilators)

* Between pillars
or doors when open which ever is the narrower

DOUBLE DECK, LOW HEIGHT BUS

9·5 m bus

Between pillars or doors when open which ever is the narrower

3. 8"

1. 8"

7' 1"–7' 5"

16. 2"–16. 3"

30. 6'–30. 10"

1. 8"

13 8' (excluding ventilators)

8 2½

SINGLE DECK, HIGH FLOOR BUS

!* Between pillars or doors when open which ever is the narrower

F

B

C

A

E

D

	11m bus		
A = 36' 1"		D = 8' 2½"	
B = 7' 4"		E = 3' 7"	
C = 18' 6"–18' 7"		*F = 2' 11"	

10m bus	
A = 32' 10"	D = 8' 2½"
B = 6' 6"–7' 4"	E = 3' 7"
C = 15' 11½"–16' 2"	*F = 2' 11"

9m bus	
A = 30' 1"	D = 8' 2½"
B = 6' 7"	E = 3' 2"–3 5"
C = 15' 11½"–16' 2"	*F = 2' 11"

A Ministry of Transport memorandum laid out the criteria for six classes of vehicle to qualify for New Bus Grant.

SINGLE DECK, LOW FLOOR, REAR UNDERFLOOR ENGINED BUS (STEPPED FLOOR)

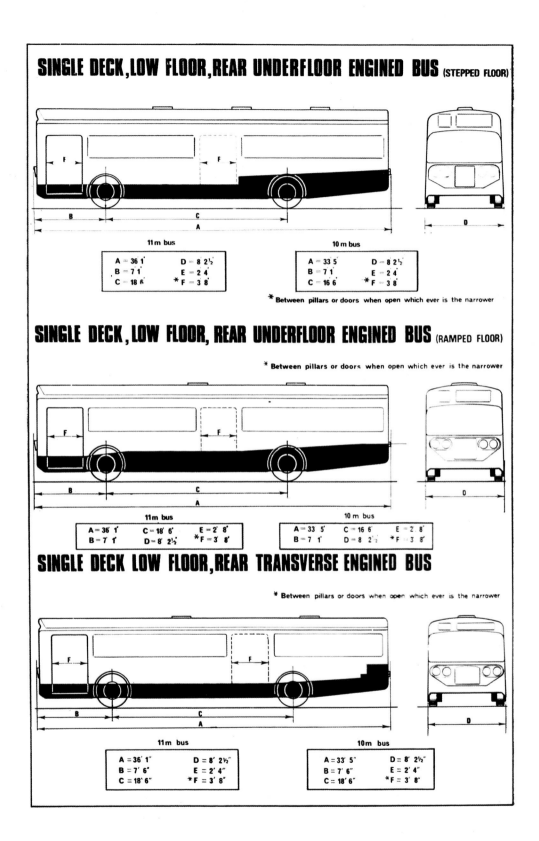

11m bus

A = 36 1˚	D = 8 2½
B = 7 1˚	E = 2 4˚
C = 18 6˚	*F = 3 8˚

10 m bus

A = 33 5˚	D = 8 2½
B = 7 1˚	E = 2 4˚
C = 16 6˚	*F = 3 8˚

*Between pillars or doors when open which ever is the narrower

SINGLE DECK, LOW FLOOR, REAR UNDERFLOOR ENGINED BUS (RAMPED FLOOR)

*Between pillars or doors when open which ever is the narrower

11m bus

A = 36 1˚	C = 18 6˚	E = 2 8˚
B = 7 1˚	D = 8 2½	*F = 3 8˚

10 m bus

A = 33 5˚	C = 16 6˚	E = 2 8˚
B = 7 1˚	D = 8 2½	*F = 3 8˚

SINGLE DECK LOW FLOOR, REAR TRANSVERSE ENGINED BUS

*Between pillars or doors when open which ever is the narrower

11m bus

A = 36 1"	D = 8 2½"
B = 7 6"	E = 2 4"
C = 18 6"	*F = 3 8"

10m bus

A = 33 5"	D = 8 2½"
B = 7 6"	E = 2 4"
C = 18 6"	*F = 3 8"

for another three or four years' extra use.

All of this stoked up demand for new vehicles to the point where orders exceeded manufacturers' — especially bodybuilders' — ability to supply on time. It required more manufacturing capacity than would otherwise have existed.

As 1980 approached, manufacturers feared that demand would fall off a cliff if the scheme ended as abruptly as planned back in 1971, but with its drawbacks apparent to HM Treasury, bus grants also looked doomed. Margaret Thatcher's Conservative government was unwilling to continue with it indefinitely, but reached a compromise to soften the blow.

It was phased out by 10 percentage point annual reductions over four years, to 40 per cent, 30 per cent, 20 per cent and finally 10 per cent in 1984, giving operators and manufacturers time to adjust. Operators stocked up with as many new buses as the grant and their funds would allow, after which demand still fell off a cliff, even if the cliff was a lot nearer the boiling sea than it would have been in 1980.

The industry that emerged from the dramatic changes that deregulation and privatisation brought immediately after this had good cause to be grateful for the vehicles bought with new bus grant, especially in its latter years. But the manufacturers — or what were left of them — endured desperately lean times while operators lived off those vehicles.

The birth of British Leyland

The manufacturer most affected by all of that change also was a product of 1968 and the actions of the Wilson government, a business that had a profound impact on the bus market but whose creation was all about cars.

This was the British Leyland Motor Corporation, which came into existence in May 1968 in an ambitious, well meaning but ultimately doomed attempt to create a UK automotive force to compete in global markets against the giants of America, Europe and Japan.

The government was encouraging bigger businesses to merge and this one brought together the Leyland Motor Corporation and British Motor Holdings (BMH), of which Leyland was by far the stronger partner, and in doing so completed a process of consolidation that brought most of the UK's heavy bus manufacturing into one business.

By 1962, Leyland owned Albion and AEC and

had diversified beyond buses and trucks and into cars with Standard Triumph; it got deeper into cars by purchasing Rover in 1966.

BMH only came into being in December 1966, a rescue by Jaguar of the British Motor Corporation (BMC), which had existed since Austin and Morris merged in 1952. Jaguar had become involved in heavy vehicle production only as recently as 1960 when its purchase of Daimler brought it a bus manufacturing business along with the luxury cars it most wanted. It got deeper into heavy vehicles a year later when it bought Guy.

Along with the Leyland, Albion, AEC, Daimler and Guy product lines, the AEC purchase had brought with it coachbuilders Park Royal and Roe, and Leyland also was in a joint venture with the state-owned bus sector.

THC owned Bristol Commercial Vehicles and Eastern Coach Works, which from being taken into state ownership in 1948 were banned from selling their products to anyone other than state-owned bus, train and truck operators. They were readmitted to the open market in 1965 when Leyland bought a 25 per cent shareholding in Bristol and ECW, and THC took a 30 per cent share in Park Royal and Roe.

THC's shareholdings passed to NBC at its formation in 1969 and by the end of the year the arrangement had evolved into a larger venture — Bus Manufacturers (Holdings) — in which NBC and British Leyland each held 50 per cent. Besides the four companies already jointly owned, they formed a new one — Leyland National — to build Leyland's all-new single-deck city bus in a brand-new factory in Workington, a facility with capacity to produce up to 2,000 vehicles a year.

These arrangements changed SBG's relationship with Bristol and ECW, especially Bristol which had supplied a proportion of its vehicles from 1954, mainly Lodekka double-deckers. One SBG director was briefly on the Bristol board after NBC came into existence, but that arrangement finished with the creation of Bus Manufacturers (Holdings).

SBG's purchase of Bristols lasted little longer, finally ending in 1971. It stopped ordering VRTs as soon as it passed from THC to STG control and

RIGHT: *An autumn 1968 advertisement from Leyland, using the impression of a Park Royal-bodied Atlantean for Plymouth to highlight — in the second paragraph — that fact that it qualifies for New Bus Grant. The same advertisement was used in early 1969, still referring to the new legislation as the Transport Bill, even though by then it was an Act.*

Leyland Atlantean now with new fully automatic gearbox

The Leyland Atlantean goes fully automatic! Britain's first double-decker to be designed specifically for one man operation now has smooth automatic gear selection. This is achieved by fitting a new control unit to the Atlantean's Pneumo-cyclic four speed gearbox. Result—silky smooth changes right through the box, with none of the jerkiness of earlier systems.

The Atlantean below, bodied by Park Royal-Roe for the Plymouth Corporation, will also qualify for the 25% Bus Grant under the Transport Bill.

Atlanteans are powered by the reliable Leyland 680 diesel, with direct air brakes for complete safety. Basic equipment includes automatic fare collection machines, an internal public address system, and Sekonik passenger computers.

So with all these features, why settle for less than an Atlantean?

Automatic control unit
Fully automatic gear selection is achieved by using air pressure valves and an electrical circuit in conjunction with electro-pneumatic gear selection valves, so that the appropriate gear is engaged as the vehicle's speed rises.

Head Office and Home Sales: Leyland, Preston, PR5 1SN, England
Telephone: Leyland 21400.
Overseas Sales:
Berkeley Square House, Berkeley Square, London W.1. Telephone: 01-499 6050.

offloaded its entire fleet of them by 1974, all but three going to NBC companies in exchange for FLF Lodekkas. It took until 1977 for the Scottish companies to be persuaded to buy any Leyland Nationals, six years after it went into production.

Unable to secure sufficient export business, the Workington plant never reached its full potential but nonetheless swelled Leyland's production capacity for most of the bus grant years. Although Albion and Guy soon ceased to make buses for the UK and some of the overlapping products were phased out, it took until 1973 for Leyland to make any significant reduction in bus production capacity when Daimler's Fleetline was transferred from Coventry to Leyland in Lancashire to make way for Jaguar cars.

Weighed down by its struggles in the car business, British Leyland became majority state owned in 1975 (it bought out NBC's share of the bus joint venture in 1982), and embarked on a series of rescue plans that by 1987 would see every bus plant close except for Leyland and

Workington. They too were gone by 1993, five years after Volvo bought Leyland's bus business.

Volvo, along with Scania, MCW and Dennis, had been drawn into the UK bus market in the 1970s as Leyland struggled to meet demand and some operators reacted against its dominance of the market.

As for the other creations of 1968, the National Bus Company (down to 15,000 vehicles) was broken up and privatised between 1986 and 1988, the Scottish Bus Group followed in 1990/91, while the PTEs lost their powers to operate buses in 1986 and the arm's length companies created then were sold to new owners between 1989 and 1994; today the PTEs in England are executive arms of combined authorities, while the organisation that began as Greater Glasgow PTE became Strathclyde Partnership for Transport.

Lip service continues to be paid to the concept of integrating public transport — offering joined up journeys between different modes — but delivering it seems as elusive in the late-2010s as it was half a century earlier.

ABOVE: *The Scottish Bus Group exchanged 106 early Bristol VRTs for slightly older Lodekka FLFs. This is one of the 10m 83-seat VRT/LLs new to Eastern Scottish in 1968, a size of lowheight double-decker that fell outside New Bus Grant criteria, operating for Eastern Counties in Norwich in 1973. It was painted in the poppy red version of NBC's corporate livery and has had its destination display turned upside down for operation in England, albeit on this occasion the ultimate destination was known only to those aware of where service 560 terminated.*

New Routemaster variety

Think all New Routemasters are red? Think again. Richard Walter illustrates a colourful selection.

B ack in 2012 when the first examples of the now very recognisable Wrightbus New Routemasters hit the streets of London, much was made of the distinctive glazed staircases. Strange then, that as orders continued to be delivered, was the introduction of all-over adverts which totally covered the glazing on many examples.

Because of the non-standard size of advertising frames carried by the vehicles, thought was given to how advertising might be encouraged. The initial batch carried eye-catching side adverts for London musicals. These proved to be popular, and by 2014 many firms were expressing interest in using the buses to advertise their products.

All-over advertising was by no means a new concept in London – it started almost 50 years ago with a Routemaster advertising Silexine paints - but the trend began of giving the New Routemasters exclusive designs which were not carried by other vehicles. Adidas was one of the first companies to make use of a series of different campaigns. Soon others followed, normally with a few buses wearing similar adverts spread across the various operating companies.

Some of the designs that have followed have been innovative and attractive, some maybe less so, but with adverts lasting in some cases only a matter of weeks, the streets of London have become very colourful and never dull. This is a selection of not only some of these vinyl wraparound adverts, but also of some special liveries, in keeping with the past tradition of original Routemaster buses on occasion carrying historic colours.

ABOVE: *LT60 is operated by Go-Ahead London and the General livery it wears is a contemporary interpretation of the colours used in the early 20th century.*

ABOVE: *LT120 of London United shows an appropriate Cadbury's advert for Double Decker chocolate bars. The design is simple but clearly recognisable as the branding for what ought to be the preferred choice of confectionery for Buses Yearbook readers.*

ABOVE: *Another London United bus, LT152, represents one of many buses in the second Coca-Cola campaign, with the bottle following the line of the glazed staircase. This livery has also been reproduced in model form by Corgi. It is in Oxford Street in December 2015.*

ABOVE: *Who would have thought it? A dating agency advertising on a London bus. That's what Bumble is, as shown on LT196 operated by Arriva London.*

ABOVE: *Another Arriva London bus, LT2, was one of the first batch of what was then known as the New Bus for London when it entered service in 2012. It was painted into all-over green when it was loaned to First West Yorkshire in 2014 which was suggesting that modern double-deckers were a better bet for the region that the New Generation Transport trolleybus being promoted by Metro, the West Yorkshire PTE. On its return to London, it retained the green livery but with gold London Transport fleetnames.*

ABOVE: *If overall adverts are supposed to broadcast a strong, simple, message, Metroline's LT654 clearly fails. Is it promoting the apocalypse? No, only awesome food, according to the message on the side. The advertiser is Deliveroo.*

ABOVE: *A smart but sombre-looking LT 253 was one of several buses that temporarily retained a black livery after the initial Adidas campaign vinyls had been removed, although the company's logo remained. This bus was operated by Stagecoach London.*

ABOVE: *London United's LT120 shows an unusual pink livery for Proper Corn snacks. Proper Corn also had buses in blue and yellow variations of this advert.*

ABOVE: *You can't argue with the wording on London United LT171, which certainly isn't one of London's 8,500 red buses. And if you're struggling to identify the product which it advertises ... it's coconut water.*

ABOVE: *Jobs. Advice. Fur. That's what's promised on the side of Metroline LT543, promoting employment agency Monster. Perhaps they should have added nightmares to that list.*

ABOVE: *LT50 was the second New Routemaster to be given a General livery by Go-Ahead London, featuring cream rather than white. It brightens up a dull day at Victoria.*

ABOVE: *Take an Aussie home for the best three minutes...? It's an interesting pitch for hair care products. LT450 is a Go-Ahead bus and shows how most adverts cover the staircase glazing, albeit with see-through vinyl.*

RIGHT: *Several buses have featured the Tommy Hilfiger chain. LT55 of London United is promoting the Gigi brand.*

All photographs by the author

Bournemouth's
YELLOW BUSES

Michael H C Baker takes a look at the evolution of Bournemouth's buses.

The elegant Hampshire resort of Bournemouth and its almost silent fleet of elegant, bright yellow trolleybuses seemed made for each other. Like all seaside resorts, Bournemouth felt the need to keep up with the latest fashions. For a while, in the immediate post-war years, when petrol remained rationed but most people were better off than ever before and there was virtually no unemployment, public transport flourished and Bournemouth was very definitely fashionable. It had always favoured the more affluent visitor, and, indeed, rather discouraged the day tripper, it's main railway station being deep in the suburbs. By contrast its art deco two-storey bus and coach station was in the heart of the town, overlooking the central park and only a few minutes walk from the beach.

Once private motoring took off in the late 1950s and then travel by car ferry and jet airliner became affordable in the 1960s, many British resorts gave up the unequal struggle and went into decline. Not Bournemouth. It continued to prosper and to follow fashion. And one fashion, which in hindsight

ABOVE: *Two Optares in Bournemouth centre, both with TYB – Transdev Yellow Buses – registrations. A Versa loads in the foreground, with an example of the relatively rare Tempo coming up behind. The 41-seat Tempo is from a batch of 11 delivered in 2009; the 38-seat Versa is one of 11 supplied in the previous year. They were photographed in 2011.*

BELOW: *Bournemouth Corporation's two-door layout was unusual, as can be seen on this 1938 Leyland Titan TD5 with Weymann bodywork. It had a sliding roof, an open section of which can just be glimpsed through the first side window on the top deck.*

if it had resisted it would today be reaping the environmental rewards, was that the municipal trolleybus was yesterday's solution to modern transport needs. The heart of the system was the Square, opposite the bus station, and the trolleybuses had been conveying both residents and visitors around the town, to Westbourne on the Poole boundary to the west, and eastwards to Boscombe, Southbourne and Christchurch, ever since replacing trams in the mid 1930s.

Evacuated to Bournemouth from our bombed house in Thornton Heath, South London, I had travelled every day to school from the town centre to Westbourne by trolleybus in 1944/45. I returned for a visit to Bournemouth once, in 1960, and the trolleybuses were all still happily going about their business, but by the time we came to live in Dorset, to which county Bournemouth had migrated, in 1977, the trolleybuses were no more, having ceased operation in 1969.

Much conspired against the trolleybus. To quote from the *Bournemouth Times* of 22 March, 1963, 'Mr Ronald Cox, the General Manager [said] a new trolleybus will cost ...about double the price of ... an excellent make of diesel double decker.' The same day the *Bournemouth Echo* noted 'rising costs and dwindling passengers... Trolleybuses have fallen out of favour...[they] cause road congestion...motor buses are far more flexible in operation, although the

ABOVE: *More dual-door Weymann-bodied Titans were delivered after World War 2, now PD2s with concealed radiators. This 1974 view was taken at the Historic Commercial Vehicle Club Brighton Rally.*

vast majority of the travelling public who use them have great affection for the trolleybus.' Few gave much thought to traffic pollution from diesel fumes.

Although electric propulsion had been in favour since the first trams took to the town's streets in 1902, the corporation had operated motor buses successfully since 1914, after a false start in 1906. Much as I liked riding in the trolleys, I was very struck by a fleet of most impressive full-fronted Leyland TD5 Titans which worked route 1 from the Square out beyond the trolleybus network, to Purewell. I persuaded dad to have a ride one

ABOVE: *'Bearing a distinct resemblance to a rectangular, cardboard box' - one of the MH Cars-bodied Fleetlines.*

ABOVE: *Alexander-bodied Fleetlines were Bournemouth's choice until 1981, with the later vehicles having AL-style bodies as shown on this 1981 bus. The bus in the background is a 1995 Dennis Lance with East Lancs body.*

evening, which all went horribly wrong for he had not noticed the sign declaring that if only travelling within that part of the town covered by a trolleybus route a supplement had to be paid. An argument with the conductor - and dad was not argumentative by nature - ensued and our ride turned out to be a very short one.

We had arrived in Bournemouth just after D-Day and the town was awash with American soldiers. This was very exciting for I'd learned from my cinema visits that America was a wonderland of modernity and to be surrounded by young men who spoke just like Bing Crosby or Roy Rogers and, quite possibly, could dance like Fred Astaire, was the next best thing to actually standing on the Brooklyn Bridge, gazing down from the Empire State Building, or riding on the Atchison, Topeka and Sante Fe Railroad. They certainly rode on Bournemouth's buses and trolleybuses. I once overheard a conversation on a number 25 and asked Mum what being 'nostalgic for home,' meant. To me these young men seemed totally grown up but, of course, many of them were barely out of their teens and might have been born and lived all their lives many hundreds, perhaps thousands of miles distant from New York or Hollywood.

Once the war was over new trolleys and motor buses were added to the fleet, 30 full-fronted Weymann-bodied Leyland PD2s of 1950 carrying on the tradition of the TD5s. At this time all double-deckers had two staircases, back and front,

and a front exit. The previous year three luxury coaches, based on Leyland Tiger PS2 chassis, were the very first post-war motor vehicles. All three eventually passed into preservation. That year 64 million journeys were made on Bournemouth Corporation vehicles. The tide, however, had reached high water mark, for at the end of May that year petrol came off the ration and the inevitable boom in private motoring was unleashed.

The next single-deckers introduced the underfloor-engine concept to Bournemouth Corporation. These were 12 Leyland Royal Tigers with Park Royal bodies, originally fitted with an open rear entrance. Six similarly-bodied lightweight Tiger Cubs arrived in 1955. A further 20 Leyland Titans arrived in 1959/60, 30ft-long buses with 62-seat Weymann Orion bodies and Midland Red type tin fronts; not one of the bus industry's more distinguished designs. Ten similar 68 seaters arrived in 1963, coinciding with the Transport Committee deciding that 'no further purchases of trolleybuses be made' and 'to discontinue the use of trolley vehicles as from a date in the future'. The last new trolleybuses were delivered in 1962, handsome Weymann-bodied Sunbeams. 301, which took up work on 12 October, was the very last new trolleybus to enter ordinary service in the UK.

Meanwhile ten more Weymann-bodied Leyland PD3 Titans became the first trolleybus replacement diesel buses in 1963. The dual staircase arrangement was abandoned and front entrance/exits would become the norm. It was

ABOVE: *It might look like an Alexander body, but this Fleetline was bodied by Weymann. It is seen operating for Bournemouth Routemaster, running in competition with Yellow Buses. It was one of 20 supplied to Bournemouth Corporation in 1965.*

inevitable that the rear-engined double-decker would appear in the Bournemouth fleet but when it did, in June 1963, few could have predicted that it would be bodied by MH Coachworks of Belfast. The chassis was Daimler Fleetline, which would become standard. Seemingly these Fleetlines, there were just two, had been diverted from Belfast to take up service in Bournemouth at the last minute. Few early rear-engined double-deck bodies were things of beauty and the MH Fleetlines were no exceptions to the rule, bearing a distinct resemblance to a rectangular cardboard box.

The last trolleybuses ran in Bournemouth on 20 April, 1969. Five months later one-person double-deck operation began in the town. By then the first of a large fleet of Alexander-bodied Daimler (and later, Leyland) Fleetlines had entered service. Alexander bodywork was relatively rare in southern England at this time but these proved to be a classic. There would be 196 of these most attractive, nicely-rounded designs, some on Leyland Atlantean chassis, taking to the streets of Bournemouth between 1964 and 1982 and their elegant looks became synonymous with the town just as had their trolleybus predecessors. Until 1973 the yellow livery had sported maroon lining but this was now replaced by blue lower panels and roof, which, whilst pleasant enough, somehow lacked the dignity of what had gone before. For a time the livery was yellow without any relief colour.

Bournemouth had little need of many single-deckers at this time, which was just as well as the purchase of 11 Daimler Roadliners proved a very bad buy and withdrawal began in 1972, just five years after they had entered service.

In 1978 Bournemouth buses started serving Poole again, as the trams had once done. This is an appropriate place to consider the relationship between the long time two dominant providers of public transport in the conurbation of Poole and Bournemouth, namely Bournemouth Corporation and, at various times, Hants & Dorset, Wilts & Dorset and More Bus.

Poole is far and away the more ancient, a port dating back to pre-history and once prominent in the fishing trade where merchants made their fortunes off the Newfoundland Banks in the 17th and early 18th centuries. Bournemouth did not exist until Lewis Tregonwell was appointed to be in charge of the Rangers keeping an eye out for Napoleon should he launch an invasion in the early 19th century. As you probably know, he didn't. But Tregonwell

ABOVE: *Between 2001 and 2005 Yellow Buses took delivery of 25 Volvo B7TLs with 76-seat East Lancs bodies. A 2003 bus with Transdev fleetname pauses by the pier in 2007.*

liked what he saw, set up home in what is now the Royal Exeter Hotel, a hundred yards or so from the sea, invited friends to stay and, hey bingo, before anyone realised what was happening you had the embryo seaside resort, which with the arrival of the railway in 1870, grew and grew like Topsy until it became the splendid watering place it is today.

The centenary of Hants & Dorset was celebrated in 2016, that of Bournemouth Corporation transport in 2002, so you can see the relationship, sometimes amicable, sometimes not, goes back a long way. By the beginning of the new millennium Yellow Buses, as the operator had renamed itself in 1982, was operating 90 per cent of bus routes in the borough, but today More is a significant presence right across Bournemouth and Christchurch, whilst Yellow Buses has increased its presence in Poole and even reached Ringwood. In 2016 it carried nearly 15 million passengers in its 131 vehicles.

There were other competitors... Charlie's Cars' routes and Sherpa minibuses were taken over in 1988, to be replaced by Mercedes minibuses. But this mode of transport has been singularly unsuccessful in Bournemouth and rapidly disappeared. Very unexpected, and most unwelcome, was the transformation of the Bournemouth Passenger Transport Association. This had custody of a number of preserved Bournemouth vehicles, kept in the council's Mallard Road depot. But in 1993 it began to operate commercial services in the town in direct competition with the Yellow Buses,

ABOVE: *An ex-Manchester Airport Dart with Pointer body passes the seafront in 2010.*

using the fleet name Bournemouth Routemaster, on account of operating former London RMs repainted in an attractive green and white livery.

Yellow Buses fought back, setting up its own low-cost White Bus operation. Standards soon deteriorated, the Routemasters gave way to a motley collection including Leyland Nationals and even some ex-Yellow Buses Fleetlines, conductors were often not up to the job, and it all came to an ignominious end in August 1994 leaving Yellow Buses victorious and the vintage vehicles homeless. A number have survived but it is sad that they no longer live in their home town. The remaining White Bus vehicles were repainted and absorbed into the Yellow Buses fleet.

During the 1950s and 1960s Bournemouth Corporation had taken on dozens of students as summertime conductors but that was all in the past and in 1986 the last conductor disappeared and all services became one-person-operated. It was around this time that I interviewed the manager, Ted Reid, who told me that most of his passengers wondered where the staircase led to and that future purchases would be mostly single-deckers. He implied, of course, that the majority of his customers were elderly and did not take to climbing stairs with enthusiasm. This struck me, even then, as on odd reading of Bournemouth, for it was rapidly shredding its reputation as the upmarket retirement paradise of the South Coast, not least because of the huge growth in the number of young people.

Wallisdown Polytechnic, known affectionately as Wally Polly, became Bournemouth University. It claimed to be the UK's best new university, and who am I as a one-time, very part-time lecturer there to dispute it. It grew enormously and is still growing, whilst language schools have proliferated. Almost overnight there was a huge increase in young people, bus services were much in demand, whilst tourists have always loved sitting on the upper deck as they sweep along the sea front or head for historic Christchurch, and so the double-decker is still a significant part of the Yellow Buses fleet.

Five East Lancs-bodied Volvo Citybus B10M double-deck coaches arrived in 1986. A nice idea, but double-deck coaches do not suit all tastes. We once hired one to take a group of children from Swanage to Beaulieu Museum in the New Forest. Unfortunately there are a lot of roundabouts between Swanage and Beaulieu, the driver had fallen out with the management and was working out a week's notice and hurled his vehicle into each roundabout with gay abandon. There were a lot of sick children.

The last of the much-admired Alexander-bodied Fleetlines arrived in 1981 to be succeeded by 20 not-much-admired, horribly, ugly Marshall-bodied Leyland Olympians. Bournemouth had always stipulated its own, unique four-piece route indicator, but no more. Ten Volvo Citybuses with very tall-looking Alexander RH bodies went into service in 1988-89, to be followed by 18 East Lancashire-bodied Dennis Dominators in 1990-92. Six East Lancashire-bodied Dennis Lances single deckers followed in 1993.

The low-floor double-deck era arrived in 2001 with eight East Lancashire Vyking-bodied Volvo B7TLs. Eight more arrived in 2002, three of them convertible to open top, continuing a tradition

ABOVE: *Recent double-deck deliveries, up to 2015, have been Volvo B9TLs bodied by Wrightbus. They seat 73.*

inscription Transdev Yellow Buses, the Transdev in a very amateurish-looking script, but against a vivid shade of yellow. The arrival of so many second-hand vehicles drew a sharp intake of breath in the town. At one time no adverts had been allowed on its buses, what was the world coming to? However the world continued spinning on its axis, even as a fleet of second-hand Pointer Darts arrived from Manchester Airport in 2007, together with a solitary Alexander Dennis Enviro400. In 2008 a solitary Dart entered the fleet but the big news that year was the welcome appearance of 11 brand-new Optare Versa single-deckers. I made a point of riding on one soon after it had entered service but this did little to enhance the financial position of the company as by then I had qualified for my bus pass. In 2009 came 11 Optare Tempos, with seven more in 2010. The double-deck fleet gained five VolvoB9TL/Wright Eclipse Geminis in 2011, and there were also two Alexander Dennis Enviro300 single-deckers.

With Wrightbus now the favoured supplier, eight StreetLite Max models arrived in 2013, followed by ten more in 2014. However there was still much need of double-deckers and 2015 saw the arrival of 12 Wrightbus Eclipse Geminis. The fleet's newest buses, delivered in the spring of 2017, are six ADL Enviro400 MMCs.

In 2009 RATP took over Yellow Buses, the Transdev bit was dropped and the RATP symbol, familiar from my many visits to Paris, now adorned the buses of Bournemouth. Through all the changes Bournemouth buses have remained, yellow, praise be, although a rather fetching shell design has been superimposed on

which went way back. More Volvos came in 2003, but this time three of them introduced the Wright body. This was the Eclipse Gemini. This remarkable firm from Ballymena was becoming an ever greater presence in Britain and would soon supply many more buses to Bournemouth. In 2004 there were six more Volvo B7TLs, three Vykings and three Geminis. In 2005 four VDL SB120/Wright Merits arrived along with another three Vyking-bodied B7TLs.

The big event of 2005 was a traumatic one, the sale of the company to Transdev. And so 103 years of municipal ownership came to an end, although 10 per cent of the shares remained with the council. In 2006 21 second-hand Darts with a variety of bodies entered the fleet, now bearing the

ABOVE: *Wrightbus has also supplied integral StreetLites, as illustrated by a newly-delivered bus in Poole in 2013. Two batches totalling 19 buses were delivered in 2013-14. The lettering above the door includes a reference to the RATP group.*

Shuttle success

Billy Nicol illustrates the varied fleet operated by Ayrshire independent Shuttle Buses of Kilwinning.

ABOVE: *Shuttle Buses started up in 1990 running minibuses, but soon graduated to bigger vehicles. Acquired from Rhondda Buses in 1996 was this Leyland Olympian with East Lancs coach body. It was originally owned by Rossendale Transport.*

LEFT: *The first double-decker was this 1976 Metro-Cammell-bodied Leyland Fleetline which had been new to London Transport. It was bought by Shuttle Buses in 1994 and operated for two years.*

BELOW: *Early additions to the fleet included a pair of Freight Rover Sherpas with rare bodywork by Aitken Coachbuilders of Linlithgow. They had been new in 1988 to the short-lived Inverness Traction company. Most Aitken bus bodies were built for local authority welfare departments. This one is in Irvine, with a Western Scottish Leyland Leopard behind it.*

ABOVE: *This Alexander P-type-bodied Leyland Tiger had been new to Alexander Northern in 1984 and was acquired in 1999 for school contracts.*

LEFT: *Operating a Strathclyde PTE tendered service in Irvine in 1988 is this smart former Central SMT Leyland Leopard with Alexander T-type body.*

ABOVE: *Two contrasting double-deckers in the fleet in 2000 were a former Tyne & Wear PTE Leyland Atlantean (left) and a one-time Tayside Ailsa (right). The Atlantean was bodied by Alexander; the Ailsa by Northern Counties.*

ABOVE: *The Laser 2 was a short-lived Duple product. This one, on a Leyland Tiger chassis, had been new in 1984 to NBC's Crosville subsidiary. This is a 2002 view. The coach, which has acquired a Duple 320 grille, wears its 18 years well.*

ABOVE: *Plaxton's Cheetah, based on the Mercedes-Benz Vario chassis, was the best-selling small coach in the early 2000s. This example, new to Boyd of Paisley, was in the Shuttle Buses fleet in 2008.*

ABOVE: *Another former SBG Leyland, following the Central and Northern examples illustrated earlier, was this Tiger with Alexander TC bodywork, new to Fife Scottish in 1985. It is seen outside Glasgow Central Station, working for First on a rail replacement service.*

ABOVE: *One of the few AECs in service in Scotland in the 21st century was this Plaxton-bodied Reliance dating from 1979. It is seen on a football hire in Glasgow in 2012. Its original owner was Cartledge of Huthwaite, near Mansfield, when it was registered DCH 359T.*

ABOVE: *A more modern coach is this MAN A91 with Beulas Stergo Spica body. New to AAA Coaches of Kirknewton in 2011, it is seen in Glasgow with Shuttle Buses in 2014.*

ABOVE: *The company runs a number of Optare Solos. Note the SBL – Shuttle Buses Ltd – registration. This was one of its first new Solos, in 2005, and was photographed in 2014.*

ABOVE: *Turas 800 coachwork by Portuguese builder Irmaos Mota (Mota Brothers) is fitted to this Mercedes Vario purchased new in 2013.*

ABOVE: *Chinese-built King Long coaches are still not that common in the UK. Shuttle Buses bought this new XMQ6130C in 2014. It is a 72-seater.*

East London Municipal Transport operated a few RT class Regents which by the 1970s were limited to peak-hour services. They had been converted to forward entrance to allow driver-only operation.

Out of Africa

There was a time when British-style double-deckers operated in parts of Africa. **Stewart J Brown** turns the clock back.

L argely because of British influence, scattered pockets of double-deck bus operation were to be found in odd corners of Africa over the years. That influence extended over seven decades. It started when Leyland shipped its first Titan TD1 to South Africa in 1928 and ended when Dennis supplied its last Dragons to Stagecoach Kenya in 1996.

Road conditions in much of Africa are incredibly harsh, and driving standards are not always of the highest. Many roads are untarred, and heavy rain can make dirt roads near impassable. That's why in much of Africa high-floor front-engined truck-derived chassis have long been used as the basis of sturdy and reliable single-deck buses.

However it's a different story in towns and cities, and the combination of good urban roads and large numbers of passengers saw British-designed double-deckers operating in various parts of sub-Saharan Africa, particularly those which had

ABOVE: *Out-of-service Leyland Titans in the Jinja depot of Uganda Transport.*
LEFT: *A Park Royal-bodied Guy Arab V of Kenya Bus Services in central Nairobi in 1972. KBS had an exclusive franchise for city services.*

been British colonies. By the time I visited Africa in the 1970s Britain's days as a colonial power had passed, but British-built double-deckers were still to be found in three of the countries I visited, Kenya, Uganda and South Africa.

Those in Kenya and Uganda dated from the 1950s and belonged to companies which were part of United Transport Overseas, a British-based business in which BET was involved and whose African interests also included significant single-deck bus operations in Tanzania, South Africa, Malawi, Southern Rhodesia (as it was then) and Zambia.

Kenya Bus Services operated city services in the country's capital, Nairobi, generally using single-deckers but with two dozen Guy Arab IV double-deckers still in service in 1972. These dated from 1956-57 and had bodywork by Park Royal and by Weymann. The well-proportioned Park Royal bodies were similar to those built for British operators, but with full-depth sliding windows. The Weymann bodies were Orions. The Kenya Bus Services business was bought by Stagecoach in 1991, and this saw double-deck buses being re-introduced to Nairobi in the middle of the decade with the delivery of 20 three-axle Dennis Dragons. Stagecoach sold KBS to local interests in 1997, but kept the Dragons which were shipped to Britain where – after various modifications including the installation of heaters - they entered service with Magic Bus in Manchester.

In neighbouring Uganda, double-deck operation had ended at the start of the 1970s, but a number of withdrawn Leyland Titans remained at the Jinja depot of Uganda Transport in 1972. These were the survivors of 15 Weymann-bodied OPD2/2s which had been new in 1956 to Kampala & District, another United Transport business subsequently absorbed into Uganda Transport. The 62-seat Titans were replaced on local services in Kampala, Uganda's biggest city, by front-engined Albion Clydesdales with locally-built 49-seat two-door bodies designed to carry 35 standees, a load which made their 0.400 engines work hard.

South Africa in the 1970s was a country where racial segregation was still government policy and would remain so for another two decades. One of the effects of this was the provision in many places of separate bus services for blacks and whites, sometimes identified by different liveries, but more often with a sign on the front of the vehicle. Alternatively, where the authorities

ABOVE: *Johannesburg Municipal Transport ran a smart fleet in dark red and cream with silver wheels and a silver roof, a bit reminiscent of Southampton Corporation. This is a 1959 Regent V with 69-seat Bus Bodies bodywork. The destination screen displays Stad/City in Afrikaans and English.*

ABOVE: *At the time they were built Johannesburg's impressive six-wheel Guy Arabs were claimed to be the biggest buses to have been built in Britain. They could carry 106 passengers.*

ABOVE: *By comparison, the BUT 9642T trolleybuses delivered in 1958 could only carry 92, of which there were seats for 73. This one is heading for Dunkeld. The board above the nearside windscreen – and repeated alongside the rear platform - advises 'Non-Europeans only'.*

ABOVE: *Johannesburg's first Fleetline was this Park Royal-bodied bus which was the last of a batch of 100 being built for the West Midlands PTE. It entered service in 1970, acting as a Daimler demonstrator.*

allowed blacks and whites to travel on the same vehicle, there were separate seating areas.

In the north of the country, the two biggest municipal bus operators in Transvaal province, Johannesburg and Pretoria, ran substantial fleets of double-deckers. Indeed, in the mid 1970s double-deckers outnumbered single-deckers in the Johannesburg Municipal Transport fleet, although

ABOVE: *Many of Johannesburg's rear-engined double-deckers carried overall advertising liveries. This Daimler CRC6/36 is promoting employment agency Manpower.*

large numbers of new Mercedes-Benz O.305 single-deckers were slowly changing the balance.

Johannesburg started running double-deckers in 1931, and would buy British-built double-deckers until the late 1970s, after which it took Mercedes-Benz O.305s with double-deck bodies until 1990 and then, from 2002, Volvo B7TLs.

The oldest double-deckers in the mid 1970s were AEC Regent Vs delivered in the second half of the 1950s. There had been 110, and most of them were still in service almost 20 years later. They were 29ft 6in long and 8ft 2.5in wide (the maximum width in the UK at that time was 8ft) and, as with most South African double-deckers of that time, had bodywork by Bus Bodies of Port Elizabeth, a company generally known as Busaf.

Perhaps the best-known of Johannesburg's buses to British enthusiasts were 30 three-axle 34ft-long Guy Arabs delivered in 1958 and 1960. These had 156bhp 12.2-litre Rolls Royce engines, at a time when a 112bhp Gardner 6LW was the norm for a British Guy double-decker, and 85-seat bodywork by Busaf. They were designed to carry 21 standees, to give a total capacity of 106. When new they had two doors, but at the start of the 1970s the rear door was removed. The high power rating was needed not just because of the vehicles' size, but because Johannesburg is 6,000ft above sea level, and the fully-laden buses had to be able to tackle a gradient of 1 in 8.

A fully-laden chassis was tested by *Commercial Motor* before it was shipped from the UK, and the tester expressed surprise at the fuel consumption when the bus made six stops per mile to simulate urban operation. The figure was 3.95mpg, meaning the admittedly bigger and heavier Johannesburg Arab was using more than twice the amount of fuel that an Arab running in Britain would consume.

Johannesburg also operated trolleybuses, and along with the three-axle Guy diesels it took 90 three-axle trolleybuses supplied by BUT (50), Sunbeam (20) and Alfa Romeo (20), all with six-bay Busaf bodies. These followed earlier deliveries of BUTs and Sunbeams. The trolleybuses did not carry registration numbers. The trolleybus system faded out in the early 1980s, despite experiments with new vehicles.

After the last of the Guys there was a gap of eight years during which no double-deckers joined the Johannesburg fleet. But it took two rare types in the late 1960s and early 1970s, with 14 Bristol VRLs and 16 Daimler CRC6/36s. All had 85-seat Busaf bodies, with authorisation to carry up to 15 standees on the Daimlers and an impressive 22 on the Bristols, taking their capacity to 107, one more than the 1950s Guys. The unusual CRC6/36s – only one other was built, for Walsall Corporation – were accompanied by ten Cummins-engined Roadliners.

The route number display on both the CRC6/36s and the VRLs was fitted below the windscreen,

ABOVE: *Johannesburg's Fleetlines carried Leyland badging, as illustrated by a 1972 vehicle on a section of bus-only road in the city centre. These buses had 89-seat bodywork by Bus Bodies.*
BELOW: *Pretoria Municipal Transport's livery was a combination of read and cream with grey window surrounds, as seen on a 1969 Atlantean with MCW-style Bus Bodies body. The moulding strip at skirt level is a nice touch. The location is Church Square, the city centre terminal for most of Pretoria's bus routes.*

ABOVE: *An advert for guys and dolls fashion gear seems a bit out of place on this old-fashioned-looking Leyland Titan OPD2 in Cape Town.*

setting the standard for subsequent deliveries. The Cummins V6 engines in the Daimlers performed no better in Johannesburg than they did in Roadliners in Britain and those in the CRC6/36s were replaced by GM V8 engines in the mid 1970s.

Whatever experience Johannesburg had with its CRC6/36s did not put it off buying more Daimlers, and the fleet's standard double-decker in the 1970s was the Gardner-engined Fleetline, albeit with Leyland badging. Between 1971 and 1976 Johannesburg bought 139 new Busaf-bodied Fleetlines, and one Park Royal-bodied demonstrator diverted from the West Midlands PTE.

Pretoria lies 40 miles north of Johannesburg

ABOVE: *Leyland badging was carried by Pretoria's 11 Bristol VRLs. They had short lives, only running from 1971 to 1978.*

and is South Africa's administrative capital. The distance and the contrast between the two was a bit like the gap between Edinburgh and Glasgow. Pretoria was conservative, staid and Afrikaans-speaking – a bit like Edinburgh, apart from the language and the jacaranda trees. Johannesburg was livelier, friendlier and English-speaking – a bit like Glasgow, apart, some might say, from the language...

Anyway, Pretoria had a tradition of running double-deck buses stretching back to the mid 1930s, although they played a less important role here than in Johannesburg. In the mid 1970s Pretoria City Transport's oldest were Leyland Atlantean PDR1s with 78-seat Metro-Cammell-style bodies built by Bus Bodies. There were two batches of 12, the first dating from 1965, and the second from 1969. The earlier vehicles replaced 1947 AEC Regent IIIs and had flat-fronted bodies similar to early British Atlanteans. The later buses had an improved front dash panel, similar to that specified by a number of British municipal fleets including Manchester, Salford and Plymouth, but with paired twin headlights.

Pretoria's newest double-deckers in the mid 1970s were 11 Bristol VRLs which, like those in Johannesburg, were bodied by Busaf. They were dual-door 82-seaters on VRL/LH6L chassis and entered service at the start of 1971, but only lasted until 1978. Where Johannesburg's VRLs had Bristol badges, those in Pretoria carried Leyland lettering. Pretoria's buses were in an attractive livery of red, cream and grey with the fleetname in English on the nearside and in Afrikaans, Stedelike Vervoer Pretoria, on the offside.

Later deliveries would include AN68 Atlanteans and double-deck Mercedes O.305s. Pretoria also ran double-deck trolleybuses from 1939 to 1972.

Pretoria was where my bus photography attracted the interest of South Africa's Bureau of State Security – the acronym BOSS sounding like an evil organisation from a James Bond film. Well, how was I to know the convoy of Leyland Olympics I was photographing was carrying employees to a government research centre?

Some 600 miles south, in Cape province on the coast of the Indian Ocean, East London was a pretty town as different from its UK namesake as could be imagined. East London Municipal Transport operated a few former London Transport RT-class AEC Regent IIIs which had been converted to forward entrance, but retained their rear staircases. By 1976 they were used solely at peak hours. ELMT operated other AECs, in the shape of half-cab Regals and mid-engined Regal IV models.

While most of South Africa's biggest cities in the 1970s had a municipal transport service there were two major exception in Cape Province, in Cape Town and Port Elizabeth. In both cities bus services were provided by a private sector business, the City Tramways group, which also had operations

ABOVE: *The first rear-engined double-decker in Africa entered service with City Tramways in Cape Town in 1960. The auxiliary red display below the final destination reads 'Whites - Lower. Non-whites – Upper'.*

in various smaller towns in Cape Province.

Of the South African cities I visited Cape Town stood out as having something of the atmosphere of a European city. As in Johannesburg, double-deckers played a significant role in Cape Town, and the oldest original examples running in the mid 1970s were 1956 Leyland Titan OPD2/9s with old-fashioned-looking Busaf bodies. These typically operated for 20 years. Small numbers of OPD2s were bought until 1960. Double-deck

ABOVE: *Over 200 forward-entrance Leyland Titans and Daimler CVG6LX/30s joined the City Tramways fleet in the early 1960s. All had fully-fronted Busaf bodies.*

ABOVE: *Cape Town's forward-entrance ex-London RTL-type Titans had an orange band to identify them to waiting passengers.*

trolleybuses also served the city from 1935 to 1964.

South Africa's first rear-engined double-decker was delivered to City Tramways in 1960, a Metro-Cammell-bodied Leyland Atlantean. It remained unique in the fleet, yet despite this enjoyed a 16-year operating life.

The Atlantean was followed by large numbers of high-capacity forward-entrance double-deckers on Leyland Titan PD3 and Daimler CVG6LX/30 chassis. All had 72-seat Metro-Cammell-style bodies by Busaf with full-width fronts which incorporated parts from their respective chassis makers' contemporary grilles. There were around 180 Titans and 40 Daimlers in Cape Town in 1975, most of them dating from the 1963-65 period.

To expand its double-deck fleet City Tramways purchased over 100 buses from London Transport between 1963 and 1966, mainly RT class AEC Regents and RTL class Leyland Titans, along with a few 8ft-wide RTWs. These served the city for around ten years. By the middle of the 1970s the survivors were all RTLs, and they were restricted to peak-hour duties. Most of them were withdrawn in 1975. Seven were rebuilt with forward entrances for one-man operation and these were identified by an orange band above the lower deck windows.

In 1970 Daimler provided City Tramways with a Fleetline demonstrator, a 12-month-old Northern Counties-bodied bus which it had bought back from Halifax Joint Omnibus Committee. After its arrival in South Africa it was fitted with deeper opening windows and flat glass windscreens. The Fleetline clearly made a better impression than the Atlantean had ten years earlier, and resulted in two orders from the City Tramways group for 25 Gardner-engined buses which were delivered in 1970, followed by a further 25 with Leyland engines in 1971. Most were for operation in Cape Town and they had 79-seat Busaf bodies. They did not last very long in Cape Town; all were transferred to the group's Port Elizabeth company in 1978-79.

The Fleetline had clearly failed to meet City Tramways' expectations and in 1974 the company took a fresh approach to double-deck operation with a front-engined model, in some ways

ABOVE: *New windows and a new windscreen don't disguise the basic look of this Northern Counties-bodied Daimler Fleetline which was shipped to Cape Town in 1970. It had been new in 1969 to the Halifax Joint Omnibus Committee and had been bought back by Daimler to act as a demonstrator.*

ABOVE: *Dissatisfaction with rear-engined double-deckers saw City Tramways work with Bus Bodies to develop a double-decker based on the proven Guy Victory front-engined single-deck chassis. The early examples had a folding entrance door in the front overhang, and a sliding exit door behind the front axle. They carried Leyland badging.*

paralleling the situation in Britain with the Scottish Bus Group and the Ailsa. The Guy Victory J with Gardner 6LX engine was a popular and reliable vehicle in South Africa, and City Tramways had been buying Victory single-deckers since 1971. Working with Busaf it developed a double-deck version, and the first of these entered service in 1974. It quickly built up a fleet of 200 which were generally operated for 16 or 17 years.

The first batch of Victory double-deckers had the entrance in the front overhang, as on conventional Victory single-deckers. Subsequent vehicles had the axle relocated to the front of the chassis, with the entrance behind the front wheel.

There are still British buses in parts of Africa – but not double-deckers. In 2012 Optare was flying the flag for British bus exports when it supplied Solos for new MyCiTi services which were being introduced to improve public transport in Cape Town.

ABOVE: *More typical of Cape Town's Fleetlines is this example with Busaf body.*

HAPPY TENTH ANNIVERSARY

Mark Bailey looks back at ten years of the Optare Versa.

Optare's stylish Versa midibus celebrated ten years of operation in the autumn of 2017. Introduced to plug the gap in the Optare range between the Solo and the Tempo, it was pitched into a market dominated by the Alexander Dennis Dart. Essentially the Versa is a longer version of the Solo, but with the door positioned ahead of the front axle to reduce the wheelbase and provide greater manoeuvrability over the longer versions of the Solo. A choice of two lengths was initially offered, 10.3m and 11m. The bodywork incorporated gently curved side windows, a tapered nose and a pronounced rake to the windscreen. A sculpted roofline sweeping down from the cab was designed to conceal air conditioning equipment if specified.

The first examples entered service with Arriva and Stagecoach group fleets in October 2007. Arriva Midlands North evaluated one at Shrewsbury and Arriva The Shires & Essex two at High Wycombe. Meanwhile Stagecoach placed its first two with

ABOVE: *In early 2008 the Transdev group received 25 Versas. These were 11.1m-long V1110 models. Nineteen were allocated to Burnley & Pendle, introducing a new livery and Starship branding, as shown by 257 (YJ57 XVU) pulling out of Burnley bus station in October 2012. Lancashire United received the remaining six for services in Blackburn. Later that year 11 similar Versas were delivered to fellow Transdev fleet Yellow Buses in Bournemouth.*

BELOW: *The fifth Versa built, YJ57 EHE, was an Optare demonstrator until acquisition by Lugg Valley Primrose in 2008. It is pictured in March 2016 at Hereford railway station, having worked in on the 501 service from Leominster.*

ABOVE: *Prototype YJ07 VRT - numerically the third Versa - is unique in being the only V970 diesel model built, and at 9.7m long is actually shorter than some Solos. It only had 120 miles on the clock when sold in 2008 to Whites Coaches of Berinsfield to operate newly-won Oxfordshire County Council tendered service 97 to Didcot. When photographed in February 2014 it was working Wantage town service 38 and still sporting its original livery.*

LEFT: *The Stagecoach group was also an early recipient of the Versa, with the first of a batch of 25 of the V1110 model arriving in late 2007. Fourteen were allocated to Red & White and route-branded for the high-frequency 151 Blackwood to Newport service, as illustrated by 25213 (CN57 BYZ) departing from a wet Blackwood bus station in April 2010. Stagecoach has amassed a fleet of around 100 Versas, with over 70 being delivered new.*

ABOVE: *Another independent to take an early Versa was TM Travel, which placed V1110 YJ08 PFN into service in March 2008. It was still in pristine condition when photographed in July 2008 leaving Sheffield Interchange on service 252 to the Crystal Peaks shopping complex. Demonstrator YJ57 EHU, the fourth Versa built, was added to the fleet at the end of 2008. TM Travel subsequently became part of the Wellglade group, and in 2014 received three V1090 models painted orange for Sheffield Line 30 work.*

LEFT: *Arriva took three V1110s for evaluation in October 2007. Arriva Midlands North 2997 (YJ57 EKE) was based at Shrewsbury, often working service 436 to Bridgnorth. It was to be 12 months before the next examples arrived, but subsequently Arriva emerged as the largest customer, receiving over 130 by 2017. 2997 had gained Wrekin Connect branding by the time it was photographed in February 2011.*

ABOVE: *Somerset independent WebberBus was an early customer for the Versa, taking its first two in February 2008. The second of the pair, YJ57 YCB, is pictured in May 2009 arriving in Taunton on service 15 from Burnham-on-Sea and Bridgwater. WebberBus suddenly ceased trading in May 2016, by which time it had received 14 new Versas, all V1110s.*

Western Buses at Kilmarnock, and 14 with Red & White in South Wales.

The appeal of the Versa was enhanced when Optare announced the availability of a diesel-electric hybrid version. In late 2010 an initial 12 entered service with First Manchester on Metroshuttle services in the city centre; this was also the first batch of Versas built to a length of 9.7m. In 2012 a fully-electric Versa was introduced, the initial three going to Travel de Courcey for Coventry Park-and-Ride duties. First has since placed electric Versas into service in York and Manchester, making it the only group to operate all three types – diesel, hybrid and electric.

In 2013 Optare announced the MetroCity, based on the Versa but with a shorter rear overhang and a more upright front. To date deliveries have exceeded 130, the largest customer being New Adventure Travel of Cardiff with 30. The uptake of MetroCity sales appears to have been at the expense of the Versa, as the only major order in 2015 was a batch of 14 dual-door examples for Manchester Airport. In 2016 a solitary order from Transdev saw 24 Versas delivered to Lancashire United and Keighley & District. Sales have however improved in 2017 with Ulsterbus adding 27 to the ten built for companion Translink fleet Metro in late 2014.

ABOVE: *The first Versas for the Go-Ahead group were 16 of the V1110 variant in 2009 for services in the north-east of England, sporting an assortment of route-branded liveries. Illustrating those for the 53/54 Saltwell Park routes is 8301 (NK09 FVB) in Newcastle city centre in April 2010. Subsequent deliveries have seen the total rise to 59, with a further ten joining the group with the acquisition of Konectbus and Anglian Bus.*

LEFT: *The first dual-door Versas were a batch of 19 delivered to London United at the turn of 2008-9, built to the shorter 10.3m V1040 length. An example is OV5 (YJ58 VBE), seen in Hammersmith in January 2013 working the 391 service from Sands End to Richmond. A further 17 identical vehicles arrived with the acquisition of the NCP Challenger operations in November 2009.*
BELOW: *In 2010 Stagecoach subsidiary Bluebird Buses received three Versa V1110s for new service 727 to Aberdeen Airport. They were fitted with additional luggage racking and sported the blue and grey Jet livery already applied to buses serving Inverness Airport. 25263 (SV60 CCX) is leaving Union Square in Aberdeen city centre in August 2013.*

ABOVE: *In late 2010 the first V970H diesel-electric hybrid Versas entered service, built to the shorter length of 9.7m. They were ordered by Transport for Greater Manchester and allocated to First Manchester. In 2011 a further six arrived for operation by Maytree Travel on services in and around Bolton. When Maytree collapsed in April 2013, YJ11 ELX was one of several reallocated by TfGM to Stagecoach Manchester. 25341 is within millimetres of grounding when seen exiting Bolton bus station in May 2013 on service 559 to Hindley and Aspull.*

ABOVE: *Marshalls of Sutton-on-Trent operate two Versa V1110s and a MetroCity. OP89 (YJ11 EKY) is passing Newark-on-Trent bus station in March 2012 working the Fosseway Flyer service 90 to Nottingham. It shows the revised arrangement for the headlamps adopted in 2011.*

ABOVE: *In 2011 Johnsons of Henley-in-Arden received five diesel-electric hybrid V1110H Versas for Stratford-upon-Avon local services operated on behalf of Warwickshire County Council. YJ11 EJK is seen in September 2011 on the park-and-ride service entering the car park at Bishopton.*

ABOVE: *The Wellglade group is another major operator of the Versa, with Trent Barton having taken 48 of differing lengths, and painted in a variety of route-branded liveries. 807 (YJ11 ENM), a V1110, is leaving Derby's new bus station in March 2012 on the Spondon Flyer.*

ABOVE: *Warrington Borough Transport purchased six diesel-electric hybrid V1110H Versas in late 2012, followed by six diesel V1110s in early 2013. The hybrid examples have graphics promoting their eco-friendly credentials, as shown by 101 (YJ62 FJO) working the Warrington Centrelink service in May 2013.*

ABOVE: *First Group operates around 60 Versas, the majority being hybrids and electrics in the Manchester and York fleets. The only diesel versions are 18 in South Wales with First Cymru, comprising nine V1110s and nine 11.7m long V1170s. One of the latter is 49301 (YJ13 HLR), pictured in Port Talbot in August 2014 in Cymru Clipper livery. Although lettered for the Porthcawl to Cardiff X2, it is working service 227 to Neath.*

ABOVE: *The fleet of award-winning Safeguard Coaches contains five Versa V1110s, all bought new over a period spanning seven years. The fourth is YD63 UZJ, seen in October 2016 arriving in Guildford's Friary bus station on the Park Barn Circular service.*

ABOVE: *Mid Wales independent Lloyds Coaches operates two Versas. V1170 YJ14 BCZ is pictured in August 2014 passing the depot in Machynlleth on the lengthy T2 service from Bangor to Aberystwyth. In 2016 Lloyds received three TrawsCymru-liveried MetroCitys for this route, which is funded by the Welsh Government and jointly worked with Express Motors.*

ABOVE: *The only Versas built in 2016 were a batch of 24 V1170s for the Transdev group. Eighteen went to Lancashire United to revitalise the network of urban services in and around Blackburn. Sporting a new Blackburn Bus Company livery and identity is 234 (YJ16 DVZ), pictured in October 2016 leaving the new bus station in Accrington on circular route 6 to Oswaldtwistle and Blackburn.*

TWENTY YEARS OF D&G

Cliff Beeton charts the progress of a Potteries independent.

D&G Coach and Bus was a late starter among the ranks of independent bus companies operating local services after deregulation in October 1986. It commenced operations in April 1998, almost 12 years later. The D&G Bus Company was named after owners Dave Reeves and Gerald Henderson, who set up the business to operate tendered bus services in the Stoke-on-Trent area. Both worked for the West Midlands Ambulance Authority, but Dave Reeves had previously worked in the bus industry, with Stevensons of Uttoxeter.

Bus services in and around Stoke-on-Trent were at that time dominated by the former National Bus Company PMT subsidiary which was now part of FirstBus as First Potteries, and which had bought up most of the old established operators of the pre-deregulation era, and seen off some newer ones as well. The time was seen as ripe for a new entrant into the game, one which would have lower overheads and could

ABOVE: *The early days of D&G are represented by a Mercedes-Benz L608D in the original all-over blue livery laying over at the old Hanley Bus Station in June 2000. 17 (D513 FAE) had been new to Bristol Omnibus in 1986.*
TOP: *Two East Lancs-bodied buses which had been new to the Metropolitan Police in 1996 were D&G's first Dennis Darts. N754 OYR is in Uttoxeter in September 2009.*

therefore price tenders more competitively.

The new company was successful in winning two tenders from Stoke-on-Trent City Council. The first three minibuses purchased to operate these were a Mercedes-Benz and two Freight Rovers in April 1998, followed by a Renault Dodge in August. Painted in a dark blue livery they were based at the former PMT depot and bus station at Longton, a cavernous premises situated under the former Jollees nightclub. By the end of 1998 the operation had increased fourfold to 16 buses.

A livery change saw the plain blue replaced with a lighter blue and cream as the fleet continued to grow as more tendered work was secured. Mercedes-Benz minibuses with various makes of bodywork continued in favour as the backbone of the fleet. The first of many Dennis Darts were two East Lancs-bodied examples that had been new to the Metropolitan Police in London. Only four coaches have ever been operated. A Leyland Swift and a Volvo B58 arrived in 2000, with two Volvo B10Ms following in 2001. They were used on schools and baths contracts, but proved troublesome and left the fleet when the contracts were terminated.

A change of policy in 2001 saw the City Council purchasing brand-new low-floor vehicles to be operated on tendered services under the Cityrider brand. The first three, Dennis Darts with Plaxton

ABOVE: **D&G Bus operated the majority of the Stoke-on-Trent Council-owned Cityrider fleet. A Dennis Mini Pointer Dart, DG52 TYU, is in Hanley in July 2003.**

Pointer bodywork, were delivered in February 2002 and allocated to D&G. They carried Cityrider livery of red, white and blue with D&G fleetnames. Further Council-owned vehicles delivered over the next three years included more Dennis Darts and Optare Solos, all joining the D&G fleet. At the end of 2003 the fleet stood at over 40 vehicles, mostly Mercedes-Benz minibuses plus the two ex-Metropolitan Police Darts and the Cityrider buses.

Optare Solos owned by Cheshire County Council were used on tendered services working from Crewe depot. This is YJ54 ZYD in Cheshire Connect livery at Crewe in May 2005.

ABOVE: *The only dual-door bus operated was 32 (P41 MLE), which was acquired with the RML Travel business. It was a significant bus, being a prototype of the low-floor Plaxton Pointer body and an exhibit at the Coach & Bus 95 exhibition before entering service with Centrewest London Buses in 1996.*

ABOVE: *Former Alton Towers Optare Tempo MX06 ADV was painted two-tone green for the 118 service between Hanley and Buxton, and given Buxton Flyer branding. Here it leaves Hanley Bus Station for Buxton in the summer of 2010, soon after joining D&G.*

ABOVE: *D&G has operated Dennis Darts with many different types of bodywork. This is a Wright Handybus, photographed at Wedgewood Farm Estate in September 2010. 12 (M67 HHB) was new to Rhondda Buses in 1995.*

With the continuing expansion of the fleet the former PMT depot at Longton was now too small, so land was acquired on Mossfield Road, Adderley Green, for a new purpose-built depot complete with offices, a workshop and plenty of open-air parking. The first brand-new vehicles purchased by the company, two Dennis Mini Pointer Darts, arrived in 2004.

Further expansion in October 2004 saw a new depot opened on a rented site in Lockitt Street, Crewe, adjacent to the railway, to service tendered work won in South Cheshire. Eight vehicles were allocated there. A reduction in the First Potteries operating licence because of maintenance issues saw D&G winning temporary school contracts requiring double-deckers. Three ex-West Midlands Travel Metrobuses were acquired for these, but they didn't last too long with the permanent tender being won by Wardle Transport of Burslem.

Wardle Transport was a new entrant to the local bus scene, previously operating only welfare buses. Over the next few years Wardle would be successful in winning tenders at D&G's expense, and consequently many of the Council-owned Cityrider vehicles would move from D&G to Wardle.

The first acquisition of another bus company came in 2005, with the purchase of Choice Travel of Wednesfield. Although run as a separate company, its attractive green and yellow buses gradually received the blue and cream D&G

ABOVE: *Three Scania OmniCitys were transferred to the fleet from Midland Choice when that operation was sold to Arriva. YN04 GMX is in Stoke on the 85 to Crewe in September 2012. The OmniCitys would later be transferred to South Lancs Travel.*

livery, and vehicle transfers between the two companies would occur from time to time.

When Arriva North West closed its Crewe depot in 2005 and transferred the vehicles to Winsford it de-registered its 85 service between Newcastle and Crewe, which was then taken on by D&G, working from Crewe depot. Successful tender wins from Cheshire County Council saw Council-owned Optare Solos, painted blue and yellow with Cheshire Connect fleetnames, being allocated to Crewe depot to work these services.

The sudden death of Gerald Henderson in 2006 would eventually see Julian Peddle, who Dave Reeves knew from his Stevensons days, acquire Gerald Henderson's shareholding in the company.

D&G won the tender for the 118 Hanley to Buxton route in September 2008 and consequently purchased its first full-size bus to operate it. The Wright-bodied Volvo B10B had been new to Keighley & District and in a departure from normal practice was painted in a striking two-tone green livery with Buxton Flyer branding.

An image refresh in 2009 would see the livery changed from blue and cream to two tone red with yellow fleetnames, and a fleet upgrading programme saw the Mercedes-Benz minibuses being gradually replaced by Dennis Darts and Optare Solos.

In January 2010 the operations of RML Travel of Cotes Heath were acquired after the company had failed to operate many of its services in the previous two weeks. RML Travel ran two commercial bus

ABOVE: *Two VDL SB180s with MCV Evolution bodies were purchased new for the Midland Choice operation at Wednesfield in 2010 but were transferred to Crewe before the sale to Arriva. This is 133 (YJ60 GGU), at Congleton, working to Biddulph Moor in April 2015.*

services, 40 Hanley to Birches Head and 41 Hanley – Newcastle - Clayton, as well as tendered services. One vehicle was acquired, a dual-door Dennis Dart SLF. RML Travel's AEC Routemaster – which explains the company's name - was not included in the deal.

In February 2010 the Volvo B10B on the Buxton Flyer was replaced by an Optare Tempo. This was again painted in the stylish two-tone green livery, and although 12.6 metres long it seated just 46 passengers. This bus was one of two that had previously worked in the Potteries with Alton Towers Transport, shuttling passengers from Stoke-on-Trent railway station to Alton Towers.

ABOVE: *Part of the agreement to buy Wardle Transport was for Arriva to repaint the buses transferring to D&G in its red livery. Alexander-bodied DAF DB250 X441 FGP is seen in D&G red in April 2015 without fleetnames, alongside sister bus X446 FGP that was staying with Arriva. The fleetnames would be applied on 9 May. Both buses had been new in 2001 to Arriva London.*

ABOVE: *Three ADL Enviro200s and one Optare Solo were given this livery for The Orange One, a service linking Meir and Newcastle-under-Lyme. Enviro200 113 (SN11 FFW) had been new to Hatts of Chippenham. It is leaving Newcastle on its way back to Meir in April 2015.*

In June 2011 it was announced that Arriva Midlands would take over the Adderley Green operations of D&G Bus. Dave Reeves said that the falling value of tendered work was instrumental in this decision. The Crewe depot was unaffected by this. Arriva took over on 9 August, and announced that it would merge the D&G operation with that of Wardle Transport at Burslem which it had purchased in October 2010. From that date it would be known as Arriva Wardle Transport and the D&G name would disappear from the Potteries. The Adderley Green depot remained in the ownership of Dave Reeves, who had agreed to rent it to Arriva for ten years. For its part Arriva agreed to extend the engineering department and add a pit and rolling road to cater for the extra vehicles arriving here.

However D&G Buses made a return to the Potteries a few months later in January 2012 when the 85 from Crewe to Newcastle-under-Lyme, which D&G had been running since 2005, was extended to Hanley via Stoke-on-Trent.

In September 2012 Arriva Midlands also purchased the Midland Choice operation from D&G. Not included in the deal were two MCV Evolution-bodied VDL buses that had been purchased new

for the fleet in 2010 and three Scania OmniCity single-deckers. These were transferred to Crewe. With funds to spare D&G would go on to purchase South Lancs Travel from its owners. It would be kept as a separate business.

An initiative in January 2013 saw the oneLink network introduced in Crewe, running from Bentley Motors to the town centre and industrial estates from 6.30am to 6pm, Monday to Saturday, and designed to make it easier to get people to work. It was funded by Cheshire East Council for two years, supported by the Department for Transport's Local Sustainable Transport Fund. Four brand-new Solo SRs with leather seats were introduced in a pink and silver livery along with a further two in fleet colours. January 2013 also saw an Optare Solo painted into Sainsbury's orange livery to operate a free service to a new store at Leek on a two-year deal. This bus was out-stationed at the premises of Robin Hood Coaches of Rudyard.

Further incursions into the Potteries occurred in June 2013 when services 94 and 94A were introduced between Newcastle, Audley and Silverdale. In September Stoke-on-Trent City Council provided a Cityrider Optare Versa to D&G

ABOVE: *Four Enviro200s were delivered new to South Lancs Travel in December 2014, but were not included in the deal to sell SLT to Rotala and were transferred to D&G at Crewe when only three months old. 32 (SL64 JGU) is seen in Newcastle still wearing SLT colours but with D&G fleetnames in May 2015.*

to operate diverted journeys between Newcastle and Hanley on route 85 via Penkhull as the 85A on Sundays and Bank Holidays. In the week this bus often appeared on Crewe local routes!

In Congleton, Biddulph-based BakerBus withdrew its Beartown network in August after running it commercially for 12 months. D&G stepped in with replacement services until the autumn of 2014 when they were put out to tender by Chester East Council and the winner was GHA Coaches.

In 2014 D&G was successful in winning the Plumline service in Stoke-on-Trent, on a tender previously operated by Arriva Wardle Transport. Two Cityrider Optare Versas were transferred to D&G to operate this. Route 33 from Westlands to Newcastle was another ex-Wardle tender success. A fourth Cityrider Versa joined the fleet in August when the 50, Hanley to Pool Dole, joined the company's growing portfolio.

An interesting transfer from South Lancs Travel in September was an East Lancs Vyking-bodied Volvo B7TL for a college contract. This was the first permanent double-decker to join the D&G Bus fleet. Initially working in SLT colours, it soon received the standard two-tone red livery.

October saw the opening of a new depot on land purchased at Cowley Way, Crewe, replacing the rented yard at Lockitt Street that had been in use exactly 10 years. This new depot housed 48 buses complete with a covered workshop, office accommodation and fuelling facilities.

A tender win outside the company's area was the 841 Stafford to Uttoxeter service for which three Alexander Dennis Enviro200 buses were purchased, the first Enviro200s in the fleet. These were out-stationed at the former Stevensons depot at Spath, returning to Crewe for maintenance.

Service changes at First Potteries in October saw the frequency of that company's service 1 from Meir to Newcastle cut from every 10 to every 20 minutes. The public outcry caused by this prompted D&G to register a new service, branded The Orange One, running from Meir to Newcastle every 20 minutes. This started on 30 October and ran free for the first three days to allow passengers to try it out. Three youthful second-hand Enviro200s and an Optare Solo were purchased and painted into an orange livery for this service. These buses, too, were out-stationed at Spath.

A rented depot in the Potteries was opened at the end of the year on the Cinderhill Industrial Estate at Longton to cater for the increase in work in the area, with the buses out-stationed at Spath and some from Crewe being allocated there. Only basic facilities and no fuelling were provided, which seemed strange at the time, but discussions already taking place, which would become known a few months later, would explain why the depot was only rented for six months.

Rumours had been rife for months about the future of Bakers of Biddulph, with suggestions that GHA Coaches was about to buy the bus services but would only employ the staff on zero-hours contracts. Luckily for the Bakers staff D&G Bus made an offer for the bus services and took them over from Sunday 11 January 2015. The deal included nine buses, a Wright Cadet DAF SB120, an Optare Solo and seven Wrightbus StreetLite WF models. Bakers continued solely as a coach operator. The BakerBus operation would give D&G Bus some established commercial work in the Potteries. At the same time D&G renumbered its 94 and 94A services as 73 and 74 to avoid a clash with the ex-

Bakers 94 which ran from Congleton to Newcastle.

Five ex-Transdev Optare Versas were acquired at this time to strengthen the fleet, along with four Alexander Dennis Enviro200s that had been delivered new to South Lancs Travel in December. The Enviro200s were transferred to D&G in exchange for three Scania OmniCitys ahead of the forthcoming sale of South Lancs Travel to Rotala.

The big news of 2015, announced on 16 March, was the buyback by D&G of the Arriva Wardle Transport operation. The funding for this was now in place following the sale by D&G of South Lancs Travel to Rotala in February. Apparently Arriva had approached Dave Reeves three times to buy back the business and the parties had been in discussion for three months. The deal would be completed on Saturday 9 May and included 19 buses, 16 Dennis Mini Pointer Darts and three DAF DB250 double-deckers. Six of the Darts had previously been in the D&G fleet when it was sold to Arriva in 2011, with five still in red livery. An agreement with Arriva would see all the aquamarine-liveried buses that were transferring to D&G repainted red before the transfer. The depot at Mossfield

ABOVE: *Six vehicles, five Optare Versas and one Enviro200, received this attractive livery for The Nines. Versa 158 (YJ57 XWB) waits at Biddulph in September 2015 before heading back to Clayton. This bus started life in 2008 with Transdev Burnley and Pendle.*

ABOVE: *The Optare Solo forms the backbone of the fleet, with over 30 of various sizes operated. This is 131 (YJ60 KFG) at Crewe on service 12 to Leighton Hospital in April 2016. The air horns and extra marker lights date from a former life with Go Goodwins of Eccles.*

Road was still owned by Dave Reeves, so for him it was a case of moving back home. From that date the Cinderhill depot closed with the buses and staff transferring back to Mossfield Road.

The ex-Wardle Transport routes that were competing head-on with First Potteries were de-registered, with Dave Reeves stating that he didn't want to be at war with them, but that he would replace journeys and routes abandoned by them. He said that he thought the Stoke-on-Trent area was ripe for expansion.

That expansion would begin in September, when First Potteries closed its Newcastle-under-Lyme garage and, unable to fit all the fleet into its Adderley Green depot, had to abandon some routes and cut back on others. D&G took on three former First Potteries routes in the Hanley area. Further cutbacks would see D&G become the sole operator on three corridors, Newcastle to Biddulph, Newcastle – Silverdale - Audley and Chell Heath – Bradeley - Hanley.

September also saw the ex-BakerBus route 9, Biddulph to Hanley, extended to Newcastle and Clayton and relaunched as The Nines. Reflecting the former BakerBus livery, five Optare Versas and an Enviro200 were painted primrose yellow with branding for The Nines.

More expansion took place when D&G won the Staffordshire County Council tenders previously worked by Bennetts of Cranberry, taking buses out to Stone, Stafford, Eccleshall and Market Drayton. On the vehicle front two brand-new Optare MetroCitys were purchased and entered service on 1 December on the 16 running from Leek to Hanley.

Finally, in December 2015, the only bus service operated by Copelands of Meir, the 40 Longton - Fenton circular, was acquired. Copelands had worked the route since deregulation but forthcoming Disability Discrimination Act regulations would make their buses unsuitable for use on local services from 1 January.

And 2016 would also prove to be a busy year. In April five routes and five buses were taken over from Routemaster Buses in the Crewe area. The company was reported to be having financial difficulties. This would introduce three new types of buses to the D&G fleet: two Dennis Darts with East Lancs bodies, two VDL Wrightbus Commanders and a VDL Plaxton Centro. The last three still wore the livery of Fishwick of Leyland, their previous owner. All subsequently received fleet livery. In July Routemaster Buses finally closed, with its remaining routes but no further buses passing to D&G. These were mainly routes running one day a week that would take buses out to Wrexham and Chester.

The big news in July, however, was the collapse of GHA Coaches. D&G successfully won the temporary tenders for the Congleton Beartown network and two other services, the 42 between Crewe and Congleton and the 87, Macclesfield to Congleton. Buses were borrowed from Central Buses and hired in to help cover the extra vehicle requirements. D&G would later gain the 42 and 87 (renumbered 99) on permanent five-year tenders, along with the 88 Knutsford – Wilmslow - Altrincham. The Beartown network was lost to Hollinsheads Coaches.

Another brand-new Optare MetroCity and a Solo SR were purchased for the 16, Leek to Hanley, service. Twelve second-hand Enviro200s and more Solos would see a start made on replacing some of the older ex-Arriva Dennis Darts. Never popular in the D&G fleet, the four double-deckers were withdrawn. Their main use had been on Stoke City football buses and on service 16.

The good relationship between First Potteries and D&G Bus would see four First Potteries vehicles being out-stationed at Crewe depot to save dead mileage on First's route 20, Hanley to Crewe. First Potteries staff would start their duties at Crewe and the buses were cleaned and fuelled by D&G.

January 2017 started with the arrival of three brand-new Optare Solo SRs for Crewe. These were in fleet livery but with green branding for route 12, The Leighton Link, that connects Brookhouse Estate with the town centre and Leighton Hospital.

Operating route 88 between Knutsford and Altrincham from the Crewe depot involved a large amount of dead mileage and could sometimes affect reliability if the roads were busy, so a search for an outstation resulted in a yard at Wincham, near Northwich, becoming active in April. Eight buses were out-stationed there to work the 88 and the 300, the Knutsford town service. Maintenance was carried out at Crewe. The company was now actively seeking more work in the area, the first sign of this being the 378 from Wilmslow to Handforth Dean which started in April.

In 20 years the fleet has increased from four to nearly 100, and D&G is now the largest independent bus operator in North Staffordshire and South Cheshire. A modern fleet of mainly Optare Solos and Alexander Dennis Enviro200s operates a mix of commercial and tendered services covering a large area from Altrincham in the north to Rugeley in the south, and from Wrexham in the east to Buxton in the west.

ABOVE: *Three Optare MetroCity single-deckers have been purchased new by D&G Bus for service 16, Hanley to Leek. The latest, 164 (YJ16 DBU), pauses at Cheddleton in March 2017 on its way to Hanley.*

Isle of Man
a return visit

John Young revisits the Isle of Man to find Bus Vannin running a much changed bus fleet.

I reacquainted myself with the Isle of Man in April 2016 after a lengthy gap. Previous visits had been to see the varied bus fleet, including elderly second-hand Leyland Atlanteans from Greater Manchester and Merseyside PTEs and Dennis Dominators from Hull. The fleet had been totally replaced since I was last on the island and a new rather uninspiring livery introduced.

ABOVE: *Wrightbus Gemini 164 (JMN 50R) was one of a minority of Bus Vannin vehicles that retained a previous livery, not dissimilar to that of East Yorkshire Motor Services. It is a Volvo B9TL and is seen passing the old Castletown brewery.*

ABOVE: *Bus Vannin Dennis Trident/East Lancs 23 (HMN 248J) is an example of the last batch of buses that remained in the company's attractive red and cream livery. At the end of the school year in July 2016 they were withdrawn, passing to Tyrer's of Chorley for further use on school services. Having previously worked the afternoon journey on school service 62 from Castle Rushen High School to Cregneash, 23 is seen here climbing away from Calf Sound on the last bus of the day, the 1620 service 28 to Port Erin. Calf Sound is one of the most picturesque points on the island. Located in the south, it is popular with walkers and tourists who come to see the seals sunbathing on the rocks.*

BUS VANNIN FLEET, 2017		
Type	Delivered	Quantity
Mercedes-Benz Citaro 530K	2016	4
Mercedes-Benz Sprinter 45	2013-16	5
Mercedes-Benz 413CDi	2016	13
Mercedes-Benz Citaro O530	2011-13	30
Volvo B9TL/Wrightbus Eclipse Gemini	2009-14	22
Wrightbus StreetLite DF	2013-14	4
Wrightbus StreetLite DF Max	2013	2
Total		**80**

ABOVE: *The current livery on B9TL Gemini 181 (LMN 181N) as it arrives in Douglas working local service 21 from Pulrose and Anagh Coar. It is adjacent to the sea terminal building on the promenade.*

LEFT: *Mercedes-Benz Citaro 223 (KMN 223U) is seen at Castletown Square on service 2A. The bus will have started out from Port Erin and will serve Ronaldsway Airport and Douglas. Castletown was the capital of the island until 1869 and is dominated by Castle Rushen, a well-preserved medieval castle.*

BELOW: *Wrightbus StreetLite DF 132 (LMN 332K) passes through the historic village of Cregneash working service 28 between Calf Sound and Port Erin. The village is dedicated to preserving the traditional Manx way of life, with original Manx thatched cottages carefully preserved.*

ABOVE: *Former UK mainland coaches on the island receive new registrations, as seen on a Tours Isle of Man Jonckheere-bodied Volvo B12M. HMN 111 was new as PN03 UCL to Shaw Hadwin of Carnforth, then served Richards Bros, Cardigan, before moving to the island. It is seen near Derby Castle.*

RIGHT: *Alongside its full-size Mercedes-Benz Citaros Bus Vannin operates a number of smaller Mercedes. Sprinter 143 (MAN 43H) sets out from Douglas on service 4 to Niarbyl via Foxdale, St John's and Peel, a journey of around an hour.*

ABOVE: *Rather more colourful than the island's buses is Manx Electric Railway car 19, seen at the Derby Castle terminus of the line to Ramsey via Laxey. It is a winter saloon dating from 1899 and built by G F Milnes. The full journey will take an hour and a quarter – change at Laxey for the climb to Snaefell Summit.*

REGRETS?
I'VE HAD A FEW

Gavin Booth ponders trolleybuses.

Friends tell me that if I'd grown up in a town or city served by trolleybuses I would have liked them more – the trolleybuses, that is, rather than my friends. They could be right: looking back I have probably got more excited by diesel buses (and, whisper it, trams) than trolleybuses. But – and you knew there would be a but – travel abroad and the opportunity to sample newer-generation trolleybuses have rather softened my views and I wish I had taken more notice (yes, and more photos) of the UK trolleybus systems in their final years.

Less than 50 miles from my Edinburgh home was the last new trolleybus system opened in the UK, in Glasgow in 1949, featuring an interesting

ABOVE: *The last batch of double-deck trolleybuses built for and operating anywhere in the world were the 50 Lancia/Dalfas delivered to Porto in 1966 and withdrawn in 1995. This one is seen in 1988.*

RIGHT: *This Daimler advert appeared in 1938, featuring a Belfast Corporation Daimler CTM6 with locally-built Harkness body, one of a number of different types that opened the system in 1938. After London Transport, Belfast had Britain's largest trolleybus fleet.*

ABOVE: *Guy chose to illustrate a range of customers in a 1939 advert, showing, from left, Rotherham, Newcastle, Llanelly and Wolverhampton trolleybuses.*

selection of double-deck and single-deck vehicles. I am ashamed to admit that I took very few photos of Glasgow trolleybuses, but do remember an Omnibus Society tour using TBS1, Glasgow's first single-deck trolleybus, and the excitement of linking two outer termini on battery power only. And just over 100 miles away was the Newcastle system which we passed through on the A1 en route to family holidays further south. My Newcastle trolleybus photo tally is just one dodgy photo of a London-style BUT/Metro-Cammell.

My London tally is even worse, given the sheer size of the system at its height: one photo of a Leyland/Metro-Cammell F1 somewhere in west London (I think), while using a Day Rover ticket to search out new Routemasters.

I do have photographic evidence of Bournemouth and Portsmouth trolleybuses, though, on a family holiday in 1961, when I seem to have wakened up to the fact that trolleybuses could actually be interesting. Bournemouth Corporation still had elderly Sunbeam MS2s with Park Royal bodies, dating back to 1934, both in closed-top and open-top forms, and I spent more of my time on these fine vehicles than on Bournemouth's quirky two-door, two-staircase, diesels. Along the coast at Portsmouth were equally elderly AEC 661Ts with Cravens bodies – but there I was rather distracted by the

ABOVE: *Trolleybus variety in Bournemouth in 1961, with, from the left, a former Brighton BUT 9641T/Weymann acquired in 1959, a 1935 Sunbeam MS2/Park Royal, and behind it a Sunbeam MF2B/Weymann – buses like this were the last new trolleybuses built for normal service in Britain.*

ABOVE: *De Lijn operated 20 of these Van Hool AG280T trolleybuses in the Belgian city of Ghent until 2009.*

1935 Leyland-bodied Titan TD4 diesels. Looking back, I realise I had A Thing about older buses.

Leafing through pre-war copies of the much-missed monthly trade magazine *Bus and Coach*, I have been struck by just how important trolleybus orders were at that time. Chassis and body manufacturers who would normally spend their advertising budgets promoting their latest diesel models used the space to sell trolleybuses instead. This was, of course, a boom time for trolleybuses (pun intended) as operators, typically municipalities generating their own electricity, switched from elderly trams to sleek, modern, quiet trolleybuses. Between 1935 and 1939 eight new trolleybus systems opened, and two more would open in the 1940s – at Cardiff and Glasgow. By 1939 there were over 3,000 trolleybuses operating for 35 systems in the UK.

Significant new trolleybus operators in the 1930s included Belfast, Bournemouth, Derby, Huddersfield, Hull, London, Manchester, Newcastle, Portsmouth, Reading and Walsall, all of whom operated them into the 1960s and some into the 1970s. I regret now that I never saw or sampled the stately six-wheelers of Huddersfield or Reading, the Mexborough & Swinton single-deckers or the odd assortment assembled by Walsall in its later days. I saw, but never sampled, the trolleybuses of Ashton, Belfast, Cardiff, Manchester, Nottingham and the wonderfully named Tees-side Railless Traction Board, but with no photographic evidence to back this.

My trolleybus awakening really came in 1985, 13 years after the UK's last trolleybus turned into its

depot in Bradford after its final journey. It was on the first of many holidays in Portugal, and my first experience of Porto's trolleybuses – older British-built single-deckers and British-style, though Italian/Portuguese-built, *double*-deckers. Porto had started running trolleybuses in 1959, and while there were newer locally-built examples, it was the British-built and British-style vehicles that attracted me, particularly the 50 double-deckers delivered in 1966, the last batch of new double-deck trolleybuses ever built. These ran on longish routes from the centre of Porto to the sizeable community of Gondomar and to the rural peace of the former coal-mining town of São Pedro da Cova. The double-deckers

ABOVE: *A 1957 Coimbra Leyland-built BUT LETB1 trolleybus with Lisbon-built UTIC body, in use in 1991, its last year in service.*

ABOVE: *Salzburg178, a preserved 1985 Graf & Stift artic, in public service on a Sunday in 2007.*

were two-door buses, initially with the entrance behind the rear axle where passengers paid a seated conductor, plus a front exit. Later these would operate as front entrance driver-only buses.

Porto's other trolleybus delights included the single-deck operation over the Douro river on the top deck of the iconic 1886 Dom Luis I bridge, a famous Porto landmark. Porto's last trolleybuses ran in 1997 but the top deck of the bridge has been reclaimed for electric traction in recent years and is now used exclusively by the Metro do Porto light rail system.

Seventy miles south of Porto you can find the university city of Coimbra, whose trolleybuses have operated since 1947. They operate still – I think. On at least one visit to Coimbra they were nowhere to be seen and I discovered that they rarely run in August, or indeed at the weekends; recent reports suggest that they rarely run at all. The fleet I first encountered in 1991 included trolleybuses on UK-built BUT and Sunbeam chassis, but now Portuguese-built Caetano/Efacec vehicles dating from the mid-1980s form the backbone of the fleet.

Other European systems have been observed *en passant* at Arnhem in the Netherlands, still the country's only trolleybus system, and Ghent in Belgium, which closed in 2009.

There was slightly more time to enjoy the Swiss systems. Interestingly, several of the surviving systems were introduced to neutral Switzerland between 1939 and 1941 while the rest of Europe was engulfed in war. With abundant hydro-electric power, Switzerland embraced trolleybuses as it did

electric railways, and at Bern (introduced 1940), Lucerne (1941) and Zurich (1939) I was able to enjoy the efficient local transport. In Austria, the Salzburg trolleybuses also operated like clockwork, including what appeared to be a preserved Graf & Stift running in service on a Sunday.

Less efficient, presumably, but arguably more interesting were the systems encountered in Italy – none of which, I am ashamed to admit, I had realised existed. On a holiday with my wife and children in Riccione on the Adriatic coast, I had expected loads of orange-painted diesel Italian-built buses. There were such animals, but also a surprise in the shape of the Rimini - Riccione trolleybus route, at the time operated by fairly new Volvo B59s which linked the two seaside resorts quietly and efficiently.

I did know about the legendary Peter Witt trams in Milan, but hadn't expected trolleybuses

ABOVE: *Still operating in Milan in 1996, an unusual four-axle 1958 Fiat 1000AF articulated trolleybus.*

ABOVE: *Rome reintroduced trolleybuses in 2005, when this Solaris-Ganz Trollino is seen arriving at the Stazione Termini on battery power.*

ABOVE: *Budapest in 2012 provided some unusual vehicles. 927 was an elderly ZiU-9.*
BELOW: *Ikarus diesel buses were to be seen in most Communist counties in Eastern Europe, but trolleybuses were less common. This is a 280.94T outside Keleti railway station in Budapest.*

too. Here was a pretty large fleet, many of them concentrated on the lengthy 90/91 outer circular route. In 1996 this route was operated by articulated buses including elderly four-axle Fiat artics on peak-hour work, 38 years old at the time.

There was a very brief encounter with Naples trolleybuses on a visit to the impressive Roman remains at Herculaneum, elderly and somewhat battered right-hand drive Alfa-Romeos.

Equally unexpected were the trolleybuses at San Remo, on the Italian Riviera. From Menton in France we crossed into Italy at Ventimiglia, just to say we had crossed the border. There were trolleybus wires above the main streets and although we waited and waited, no trolleybuses appeared. We sussed that this must be the 18km route down the coast to San Remo, but only diesel buses appeared to be running on it.

Then, about to abandon the search in favour of some pasta and a glass of vino, a trolleybus appeared. We jumped aboard, expecting to pay the driver, but this was not the way. We needed pre-paid tickets and, bless him, the driver took our money, stopped at a nearby *tabacchi* and emerged with our tickets. Although we encountered no more trolleybuses en route to San Remo, once there we found more, working town services.

The least expected Italian trolleybuses were probably those discovered in Rome, but unlike Ventimiglia there were no wires to provide the

clues. Outside Stazione Termini, the city's main railway station, were articulated Solaris buses in a green livery, and closer inspection revealed trolleybus booms flat on the roof. This prompted the inevitable trip and once clear of the main city centre, running on battery, it was intriguing to see the start of the wiring; at a designated spot, the bus stopped and the driver pressed a button for the booms to meet the wires for the rest of the journey.

My most recent trolleybus encounter, in 2012, was in the Hungarian capital of Budapest where trams are the most prominent form of public transport. Just beyond the imposing Hungarian Parliament Building is a trolleybus terminus, served then by an interesting selection of vehicles. Some were locally-built Ikarus types, but by far the most interesting were elderly Soviet-built ZiU-9s looking as if they hadn't received much attention since they were built. The term 'rust-bucket' came to mind and they looked so dreadful that a trip was essential. Inside they were just as bad with deeply-ingrained dirt and missing panels, but while the bodywork may have been neglected, they were no slouches when they set off into traffic.

The only trolleybuses I have encountered beyond Europe were in the United States, in Boston – or more precisely Cambridge where, after sampling the delights of real PCC cars on the tramway, I crossed the Charles River to discover trolleybuses in the Harvard Bus Tunnel where passengers board on the left-hand side of the buses, explaining the wide doors on both sides.

My son Andrew, a deputy head teacher, sets off every couple of years to exotic places on character-building trips with senior pupils. In 2012 he was in Mongolia and in its capital, Ulan Bator, he discovered and photographed trolleybuses for his old dad. Buses are not his thing, so, like me, he had no idea what he was photographing. Not surprisingly, they turn out to be Soviet-built ZiU-9s, the type built in vast numbers between 1972 and 1992; the excellent *World Trolleybus Encyclopaedia* suggests around 45,000 were built.

You can still ride on trolleybuses in Britain, of course, notably at the National Trolleybus Museum at Sandtoft, near Doncaster (though strictly in Lincolnshire), and the East Anglia Transport Museum at Carlton Colville near Lowestoft. Both are fine museums – Sandtoft dedicated to the trolleybus and Carlton Colville taking a wider view of transport – and both are well worth visiting. At Sandtoft I

ABOVE: *At the National Trolleybus Museum at Sandtoft, former South Shields 204, a 1937 Karrier E4 with Weymann body.*

was given the opportunity to *drive* a trolleybus, an altogether more complicated experience than driving a diesel bus, certainly for this rookie. There is also what is apparently the longest regular trolleybus route remaining in Britain, the 0.8-mile route at the excellent Black Country Living Museum at Dudley,

On many of the surviving trolleybus systems mentioned here, the buses themselves have been replaced by newer models, some with more than a passing resemblance to modern trams – a deliberate move, no doubt, as for many countries a tramway is seen as the ultimate symbol of a modern transport system, with the trolleybus in second place and the considerably cheaper and more flexible motorbus in third place.

But while trolleybus systems around the world are investing in new and technically advanced vehicles, it seems unlikely that the UK is going to witness a trolleybus renaissance. South Yorkshire PTE commissioned a double-deck trolleybus that emerged in 1985 as a bus based on the PTE's standard diesel type, an Alexander-bodied Dennis Dominator, but with a 300kW traction motor and a small electric generator. It was tested under a short section of overhead in Doncaster but the experiment was discontinued and the bus can now be seen and sampled at the Sandtoft museum.

Leeds, after it was denied its proposed Supertram in 2005, decided to have a second shot with its £173.5million NGT (New Generation Transport) trolleybus scheme. But in 2016 this too was knocked back – a pity, because it had the hallmarks of a well thought-out scheme that might have aroused fresh interest around the country.

Even from me.

ABOVE: *Glasgow's last new double-deck trolleybuses were 90 of these attractive BUT 9613T with Crossley bodies, delivered in 1957-59. TB78, preserved at the National Trolleybus Museum, is seen in 2001.*
BELOW: *South Yorkshire PTE's 1985 experimental Dennis/Alexander trolleybus, named Electroline and now at the National Trolleybus Museum.*

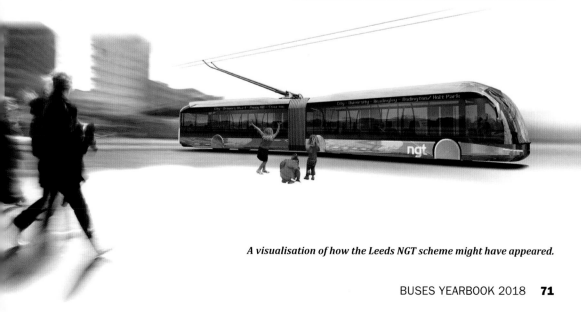

A visualisation of how the Leeds NGT scheme might have appeared.

IPSWICH BUSES

A LOCAL AUTHORITY SURVIVOR

Ipswich Buses is one of the few remaining British bus operations still owned by a local authority. **Geoff Mills** illustrates how the fleet has changed over the last three decades.

ABOVE: *Between 1974 and 1977 Ipswich Borough Transport bought 40 generally similar Leyland Atlanteans with two-door bodies by Roe of Leeds. This 1976 bus was acquired by the Ipswich Transport Museum in 1994, and is seen in 2000 outside the museum in the former Priory Heath trolleybus depot.*

ABOVE: *Some out-of-town services have been operated by coaches, such as this 1979 Bedford YMT with Plaxton Supreme bodywork which was purchased in 1988 from local operator Bickers of Coddenham, and carried Suffolk Bus names. It was new to Rochester & Marshall of Great Whittington, Northumberland.*

ABOVE: *Between 1983 and 1989 Ipswich bought 25 new Dennis Falcons, of which 18 had two-door East Lancs bodies. This bus photographed in the Old Cattle Market was new in 1985 and was named Ardwina.*

ABOVE: *As well as buying Falcons, Ipswich bought two Dennis Dominators. The first was delivered in 1985 and had two-door East Lancs bodywork with 70 high-backed seats.*

ABOVE: *Three Volvo Olympians in 1995 had East Lancs bodies which were similar to the Alexander R-type. This is a 2003 view in Crown Street.*

ABOVE: *Four Optare Deltas, based on DAF SB220 chassis, were delivered in 1994. They were two-door 44-seaters. By this time Ipswich was one of very few operators outside London still buying two-door buses. This one is seen when new.*

ABOVE: *This standard NBC-style ECW-bodied Leyland Olympian was purchased from Trent in 1998, at which time it was 13 years old. It still looks smart in this 2002 view.*

ABOVE: *To mark the centenary of municipal transport in Ipswich this DAF DB250 was delivered in a gold livery. It is a DAF DB250 with East Lancs body, one of six bought in 2002-03.*

ABOVE: *Four Optare Excels were delivered in 2002, following ten supplied in 1997. The 2002 vehicles were long-wheelbase L1180 models with 42 seats and carried a distinctive livery for a park-and-ride service.*

ABOVE: *In 2003 this Leyland Olympian with Alexander (Belfast) body joined the fleet. It was new in 1990 to Dublin Bus.*

ABOVE: *Six Dennis Dart SLFs with 35-seat Alexander ALX200 bodies were bought from Stagecoach London in 2012, and were in the new green and purple livery introduced that year. They dated from 2001.*

ABOVE: *New buses in 2013 were four Alexander Dennis Enviro200 39-seaters. They were followed by another in 2014, and then by eight in 2016.*

ABOVE: *Four Transbus-built Super Pointer Darts were acquired from Lothian Buses in 2015. The Super Pointer Dart was the biggest member of the Pointer Dart family, with 42 seats.*

ABOVE: *In May 2016 Ipswich Buses took over the ten-vehicle business of Carters Coach Services of Capel St Mary. The newest bus in the fleet was this unusual combination of VDL SB180 chassis and MCV Evolution body.*

ABOVE: *Operating on a former Carter's service in June 2016 is this ex-Stagecoach East London Dennis Trident with Alexander ALX400 body. It was new in 2001 and was bought by Ipswich Buses in 2012.*

BRADFORD CORPORATION'S
LONDON RTs

Stuart Emmett explores the period when 25 ex-London Transport RTs
served his native city.

I n 1958 Bradford Corporation Transport
had a problem. It was still running 27 utility
double-deckers, and they had to be replaced.
These were 12- to 15-year-old DKY-registered
Daimler CWA6s with 56-seat bodies by Duple
(19), Brush (six) and Northern Counties (two).

These utilities would have been recertified after
seven years when their initial Certificates of Fitness
expired (between 1951 and 1953), then again for
five years between 1956 and 1958, and thereafter
every three years at most. So 1959 was to be the
start of the third series of re-certifications.

Clearly the cost of re-certification was looked at,
and instead of extending the lives of the Daimlers,
a decision was taken to buy 25 London Transport
RT-class AEC Regent IIIs dating from 1947 from
Birds, the dealers in Stratford-upon-Avon. Birds
had bought many RTs from London, selling them
on to a variety of other operators. Bradford had a
history of buying second-hand trolleybuses, these

would be its first major second-hand motorbus
purchases. And it was no stranger to the Regent III,
having bought 100 between 1947 and 1953; those
delivered in 1953 were the fleet's newest buses.

In February 1958 former London Transport RT418
(HLX 235) was brought up to Bradford where it
was checked over and evaluated. Following this
25 were bought, with the DKY-registered utilities
going to Birds in part exchange plus £1,700 per
bus. This was a lot cheaper than buying a brand
new bus, which cost around £6,000 in 1958.

The 25 RTs were 11 years old and were numbered
by Bradford as 401 to 425 in a logical sequential
registration order, apart from two of the last to

enter service (411 and 425) that were out of sequence. Perhaps these two were substitutes for vehicles which had been originally expected.

The buses started to arrive in Bradford from March 1958 and after quick attention to changing indicators and livery, the first six entered service on 10 May. They were quickly followed by another 14 between 16 May and the 6 June, one on 1 July and the final four on 1 August. The lateness in entering service of the last four could have been down to the annual Bradford two-week summer holiday when the city effectively closed down; these four were also the last sent in June from London Transport to Birds.

Meanwhile all of the DKY-registered utilities had been withdrawn by 31 May 1958, apart from one which stubbornly held on until 17 July.

What was special about the RT?

The RT was truly a classic bus but with an enigmatic name; what did RT really stand for? The debate argued over Regent Type, Revised Type or Regent Three. There were over 7,000 built (if we include the Leyland RTL/RTW family), with a maximum of 6,180 in service at any one time. The degree of design standardization was high, with only relatively minor variations between the four body builders and the two chassis builders. This enabled high interchangeability at overhaul.

The overhauls were initially undertaken at London Transport's Chiswick Works but between 1952 and 1955 this work was progressively moved to a new overhaul factory that was formally opened in 1956 at Aldenham, north of Edgware. This site had been intended to house an Underground train depot for an extension to the Northern Line that was never built.

In the early 1950s many of the early RTs with route number displays mounted on the front dome – giving rise to the description "roof box" for such bodies - received overhauls at Chiswick without body exchanges, however by 1956 Aldenham was ready. Up to 50 buses could be handled each week.

The chassis and body were separated for overhaul and such high interchangeability meant that the body on an RT after overhaul was not always the one that was fitted when it had arrived. Indeed a float of bodies was always in reserve, and whilst most of the Bradford RTs had entered service in London with the early roof box bodies (type RT3), some were received at Bradford with the later non roof box bodies (type RT8). This was because as the early 1947 buses were going in for their second overhaul, the newer buses went for their first; so early RT3 roof box bodies

ABOVE: *Typical of the buses which the RTs replaced is 1943 Duple-bodied Daimler CWA6 478 (DKY 478).* PM Photography
BELOW: *This is how the RT8-style bodies, without the roof box, looked when new, with the route number alongside the destination displays. RT 885 (JXN 263) was bodied by Park Royal in 1948 and has a body which was coded RT3/1.* Park Royal

started to appear on some later chassis, and newer RT8 bodies, where the route number was displayed alongside the destination, appeared on earlier chassis.

Production of the RT had run from 1939 to 1942 when it was halted by the war after 151 had been built. Production re-started in 1947 and continued up to 1954. By this time the passenger climate had changed, and the last ones were stored and finally entered service in 1958. London Transport simply had too many buses. Following the sale of the 120 non-standard Cravens-bodied RTs in 1956, the first 50 standard but surplus RTs were sold in 1958 via Birds, including the 25 which went to Bradford. These sales were of early postwar RTs with HLW

HLX 238

90

HLW 157

BRADFORD'S RTS, ALL ENTERED SERVICE IN 1958

Fleet No	Registration	Body
401	HLW 141	Weymann
402	HLW 143	Weymann
403	HLW 145	Weymann
404	HLW 148	Park Royal
405	HLW 149	Weymann
406	HLW 150	Park Royal
407	HLW 152	Park Royal
408	HLW 155	Park Royal
409	HLW 158	Weymann
410	HLW 159	Park Royal
411	HLW 157	Saunders
412	HLX 161	Park Royal
413	HLX 164	Park Royal
414	HLX 223	Park Royal
415	HLX 229	Park Royal
416	HLX 230	Park Royal
417	HLX 231	Weymann
418	HLX 232	Park Royal
419	HLX 233	Park Royal
420	HLX 234	Park Royal
421	HLX 235	Saunders
422	HLX 238	Weymann
423	HLX 241	Weymann
424	HLX 243	Park Royal
425	HLX 228	Weymann

ABOVE: *422 (HLX 238) with an RT8 body (left) and 411 (HLW 157) with a roof box RT3 body at Thornbury and ready to go in service in August 1958 in overall blue livery.* PM Photography

and HLX registrations but, because of the Aldenham system, although they were the oldest chassis they did not necessarily have the oldest bodies.

In London, 22 of the RTs purchased by Bradford had been allocated from new to Leyton depot in the east of London, while the other three had operated from Croydon in South London. Whilst at Leyton one of their main routes was the 10. This ran daily between Abridge (Blue Boar) and London Bridge Station via Chigwell, Woodford Bridge, South Woodford,

ABOVE: *418 (HLX 232) showing the dull "rush it into service" livery, that blends in with the grimy buildings - a product of many years of coal-fired boilers in the local textile mills.* Online Transport Archive/Harry Luff

Wanstead, Leytonstone, Stratford, Bow, Mile End and Aldgate. It was extended on Mondays to Saturdays (except evenings) to Victoria Station via St George's Circus, Lambeth Bridge and Horseferry Road; and extended on Sundays to Elephant & Castle. It was a 90-minute journey from central London to Abridge.

RTs in service at Bradford

As mentioned, whilst all the Bradford RTs had entered service in London with roof box bodies, some were received at Bradford with non roof box bodies following body changes at Aldenham.

Also, according to J S King's lovely 1995 book, *Bradford Corporation Motorbuses*, the RTs came from Birds with a five-year Certificate of Fitness, which meant they now had a certification-free life until 1963.

In its desire to get them into service as quickly as possible, Bradford gave them a quick one coat over-paint in blue, with the narrow London style single cream band retained. A slight exception was with 425, one of the last to enter service, which had cream around the upper deck windows in the pre-1950 London Transport style.

The roof box number indicator was used where fitted, and the "via" part of the main front destination display paneled over, leaving a small aperture for the final destination, for which Bradford had ordered new blinds.

On the RTs that did not have a roof box and therefore had the wider final destination indicators, the ultimate destination aperture was left, but narrowed, and in the middle space above, a route number blind was fitted. The rest of the front aperture was then merely over-painted.

The destination indicators above the platform were over-painted on some buses, although on others the bottom part was used to show the final destination. The rear indicators were similarly over-painted leaving a small square for a route number blind.

The end result was buses with two different frontal styles and unfortunately in their deep overall blue they all looked rather bland and drab when compared to the normal Bradford blue livery with cream window surrounds on both decks.

401 (HLW 141) was one of the last RTs to be withdrawn in 1969. It is seen in September 1963 coming out of the town centre onto Leeds Road. Alistair Douglas

The Bradford RTs settled down to work from the Ludlam Street depot in the city centre. As this was the main motorbus depot, the RTs could appear on any route from there, especially at peak times. However they were commonly found operating on the Otley Road routes.

From 1960 onwards, when it became time for the Bradford standard 50,000-mile overhaul and repaint, all the RTs were painted into the full Bradford standard colours. Many also had the roof box removed and standard Bradford destination displays fitted.

Final years at Bradford

The RTs were good servants in Bradford but they eventually had to go, with five withdrawn in 1963. These were followed by three in 1964, two in 1967, 11 in 1968 with the final four in April 1969; a service life in Bradford of between five and 11 years.

Their replacements were varied, as in the years from 1963 to 1969 Bradford received 180 new buses. These were AEC Regent Vs, Daimler CVG6LXs, Leyland Titan PD3As, Leyland Atlantean PDR1/3s and Daimler Fleetline CRG6LXs. Some of these replaced trolleybuses, but they also replaced most of the Regent IIIs bought new by Bradford, and most of the fleet's early postwar Leyland Titans, as well as the RTs.

ABOVE: *Also in September 1963 amidst street furniture is 410 (HLW 159) after being painted into full Bradford livery with cream window surrounds, and still with its roof box route number display.* Alistair Douglas
BELOW: *412 (HLW 161) originally entered service with a roof box but in this view has been rebuilt with the standard Bradford destination display. Just visible on the left is 425 (HLX 228), still in the mainly blue livery, and showing how the rear destination indicators were originally over-painted leaving space for the route number. The location is Church Bank, which leads off the end of Forster Square.* PM Photography

LOOKS FAMILIAR?

Sholto Thomas looks at buses in the USA with British connections.

ABOVE: *From 2001 a link between Wrightbus and Chance Coach saw buses being built in the USA with bodywork to Wrightbus designs. Chance subsequently became Optima Bus, and the bus was marketed as the Optima Opus. This example seen in Lancaster, Pennsylvania, in 2008, is operated by the appropriately-named Red Rose Transit.*

ABOVE: *Awaiting custom in June 2012 are these Optima Opuses at the West Visitor Center in Glacier National Park, Montana. At several National Parks in the USA buses provide internal transport because not all areas are accessible to private cars to reduce congestion or to address environmental issues.*

ABOVE: *In Ohio the Greater Cleveland Regional Transit Authority runs Optimas disguised to look like vintage trolley cars, with a fake clerestory roof, a wire mesh front lifeguard and slatted wooden seats. They operate a free service around the centre of Cleveland, as seen here in 2015.*

ABOVE: *Stagecoach's Megabus brand has a strong presence in parts of the USA. Here a Van Hool Astromega pauses for a refreshment break at Barstow, California, on the M10 service from Las Vegas to Los Angeles, a 270-mile, five-and-a-half hour, trip.*

ABOVE: *No fewer than 141 Alexander Dennis Enviro500 double-deckers operate in Las Vegas, Nevada. However, not all run on the high-profile Deuce route downtown. This example in plain livery is on a 15-mile North-South route in the east of the conurbation in April 2015. The Enviro500s are operated by the Regional Transportation Commission of Southern Nevada.*

ABOVE: *From 2000 to 2005 Optare was owned by North American Bus Industries. As a result a small number of 31ft-long Solos were sold in the USA as the NABI 30-LFN. This one is operating for City Sights in Salt Lake City, Utah, in 2015, proclaiming that it is providing "Our city's finest tour".*

ABOVE: *This Thomas-Dennis SLF200, appropriately for an Alexander design, is on the downtown Dash service in Grand Rapids, Michigan. It was photographed in the summer of 2016. The bus was produced in an agreement between Thomas Built Buses and Dennis.*

ABOVE: *A Thomas-Dennis SLF200 of Lextran, the local transit authority in Lexington, Kentucky, in 2006. The SLF was built in the USA from 1999 to 2007, latterly with a Mercedes-Benz engine by DaimlerChrysler which took over the Thomas business in 2003.*

ABOVE: *A Grand Valley Transit SLF200 with its front-mounted bicycle rack in use, passing the railroad station in Grand Junction, Colorado, in 2009.*

All photographs by the author.

FIVE YEARS
ON THE HAMMERSMITH ROAD

I n late autumn 2011 my then employer closed its Chichester office and offered me a transfer to London; Brook Green, W6, to be precise. It was not ideal but was paid employment, albeit something I considered a short-term option while seeking an alternative closer to home. Little did I realise that aim would take almost five years to achieve.

A daily commute from my south coast home was not the most feasible travel option but my mother-in-law very kindly offered weekday lodgings in Eltham, SE9. Readers with a geographical knowledge of London's public transport will know there are numerous ways to travel between the south-east and the west. South Eastern Trains took care of the Eltham to Charing Cross leg

An employment change in summer 2016 brought **David Jukes'** regular commute on London's route 9 buses to a close. He describes his experiences of one of the capital's shortest trunk routes.

ABOVE: *The 9 was allocated LT-class New Routemasters from October 2013; these usually worked in crew mode during weekday morning and afternoons as shown here – the open rear platform is the clue (rear doors were closed between stops when the bus was driver-operated). LT85 (LTZ 1085) contrasts with traditional Routemasters in Kensington High Street on 6 March 2014.*

of the trip, but what about the remainder?

The District Line from Embankment to Barons Court obliged for a short time before the costs of peak-hour Underground travel became all too apparent and a cheaper alternative sought. It eventually dawned on me the door-to-door journey between Charing Cross and Brook Green could be undertaken using the number 9 bus route in much the same time as the train; the longer bus ride mitigated by shorter walks at both ends.

A brief history

The 9 is one of Transport for London's shortest trunk routes and one of the capital's earliest. It traditionally ran between Mortlake and Liverpool Street via the current 209, 9 and 11 routes with Sunday extensions to Romford, Becontree Heath and Aldgate at various times in its history.

Central Area changes in July 1992 saw the 9 cut back at its eastern end to Aldwych simultaneously with the imposition of a weight restriction on Hammersmith Bridge – henceforth barred to double-deck buses. So the 9 was curtailed at

ABOVE: *Tower Transit acquired First Group's London operations in June 2013, the new owner quickly applying their identity to the heritage route 9 Routemasters - the logo is above the first lower-deck side window. RM1204 (204 CLT) has just departed its Kensington terminus on 13 February 2014 and will run light via Holland and Addison Roads to stand alongside the bus stop on the opposite side of the road.*

ABOVE: *First London's SRM3 (650 DYE) – originally RM1650 – had its Queen's Silver Jubilee livery modified to include a white vertical stripe and Olympic-themed bullseyes to celebrate the 2012 London Games award. The bullseyes were removed before the Games to leave this livery variant as seen in Kensington High Street on 3 May 2013 approaching its Holland Road terminus.*

ABOVE: *Still wearing the company's original grey and red livery is London United VR227 (BD51 YCS), a 2002 Wright Eclipse Gemini-bodied Volvo B7TL, operating a morning peak route 49 journey at the western end of Kensington High Street on 16 May 2012. This route runs alongside the 9 between Holland Road/Addison Road and Palace Gates, Kensington.*

ABOVE: *Transport for London's livery requirements initially saw London United buses receive a simplified livery of overall red with a grey skirt before plain red prevailed. Catching the early morning sun in Kensington High Street is SLE46 (YN55 NKR), a 2005 East Lancs OmniDekka-bodied Scania N94UD. Route 27 shares the 9's route between Hammersmith Bus Station and Kensington Church Street.*

ABOVE: *London United SP153 (YP59 OEM), a 2010 Scania N230UD OmniCity operates an early evening route 10 journey through Kensington High Street on 2 May 2013. The 10 shares Hammersmith Bus Station terminus with the 9 and operates alongside it from there to Hyde Park Corner.*

ABOVE: *The Kensington Olympia stop in Hammersmith Road is served on 3 September 2015 by London United ADH27 (YX62 FFB), a 2013 Alexander Dennis Enviro400H hybrid. Overtaking Tower Transit VNW32404 (LK04 HXP), a 2004 Wright Eclipse Gemini-bodied Volvo B7TL acquired with the First London business, will turn left into North End Road and makes its Olympia stop there.*

ABOVE: *Route 360 terminates at the Royal Albert Hall and runs alongside the 9 between Exhibition Road and Queens Gate. Go Ahead London WHY12 (LX11 DVG), a 2011 Wrightbus Electrocity, approaches the latter junction on 12 June 2015.*

Hammersmith and a new Dart-operated route 9A introduced Monday to Saturday daytimes between Mortlake and Kensington. The Darts also operated a route 9 between Mortlake and Aldwych on evenings and Sundays.

March 1997 saw the 9 standardised as a daily Hammersmith to Aldwych operation and the 9A replaced by daily route 209 between Mortlake and Hammersmith. This remains the case today although the 9 was diverted from Piccadilly Circus to serve Pall Mall and St James's Street from February 2012.

The vehicles
Crew operation on the 9 ceased on 4 September 2004 with its transfer from Shepherd's Bush Garage to Stamford Brook; VLE-class East Lancs Myllennium Vyking-bodied Volvo B7TLs replaced the previous AEC/Park Royal Routemaster and MCW Metrobus allocations. The Volvos held sway until 26 October 2013 when the 9 received a daily allocation of LT-class New Routemasters.

Shadowing the Volvos and New Routemasters between 12 November 2005 and 25 July 2014 were Marshall-refurbished Routemasters operating the heritage route 9. This initially linked Aldwych and Kensington, Prince Consort Road, (for the Royal Albert Hall) before its revision to run between Trafalgar Square and Kensington, Holland Road, from 13 November 2010. It was also diverted via Pall Mall from February 2012.

It was most noticeable how bus stop dwell times reduced when the New Routemasters replaced the Volvos – an advantage of three doors and two staircases compared to two and one respectively. The former also had more than their fair share of teething problems – I experienced a handful of breakdowns during the New Routemasters' first year or two which necessitated a change onto a following bus. The New Routemasters' heating and ventilation system was most noticeably ineffective during wet or hot weather; the resulting condensation, stuffiness or extreme heat could not be easily addressed thanks to a lack of opening windows. Fortunately the seats were more comfortable

ABOVE: *Approaching the Addison Road junction with Kensington High Street on 13 February 2014 is First Berkshire 37985 (BJ11 XGY), a coach-seated Wright Gemini Eclipse-bodied Volvo B9TL, working Green Line route 702 from Victoria to Bracknell.*

ABOVE: *The lack of availability of a coach required the operation of First Berkshire 33179 (LR02 LYY), a 2002 Plaxton President-bodied Dennis Trident new to CentreWest as its TN1179, on Green Line 702 on 17 October 2015.*

than those fitted by East Lancs in the Volvos – there seemed to be a shortage of padding in certain quarters during the noughties. However, to compensate, large windows with opening sections were fitted which give an excellent (and ventilated) view of the outside world.

The route

So do please join me on a typical morning journey to work. The Eltham train arrives at Charing Cross around 06.36hrs, six minutes before the first westbound 9 is due to depart from its stop by the station forecourt in the shadow of Queen Eleanor's Cross.

We may strike lucky and immediately board a late-running last N9 journey but lucky is a relative term. Passage may be swift (I recorded my fastest station to office journey on an N9) but uncomfortably so owing to the route's SP-class Scania OmniCity allocation. SP may officially stand for Scania Poland but could equally be an abbreviation for spartan – the interiors being somewhat rudimentary and clinical (and the seats very hard). Sole entertainment is watching passengers familiar with the New Routemaster

boarding through the Scania's centre doors and trying to tap in with their Oyster cards...

Strand is served by nine other routes which can make identifying a 9 slightly tricky at a distance (it was easy when the New Routemasters were introduced as the 9 was the first Strand route to receive them). We board our New Routemaster at the rear, exchange brief pleasantries with the platform assistant as we tap in before climbing the back staircase to take an upstairs seat – the best way to travel.

With everyone on board, the usually half-full New Routemaster takes us past the equestrian statue of King Charles I, isolated on a roundabout at Trafalgar Square's south side from Admiral Lord Nelson, Major General Sir Henry Havelock and General Sir Charles James Napier – all standing firm in the main square. We stop opposite the Canadian High Commission in Cockspur Street to pick up more passengers – this is a useful interchange with northbound routes from Whitehall.

The Athenaeum passes to the left as we head into Pall Mall and lose the other parallel bus routes which all turn right into Regent Street. The 9 has Pall Mall and St James's Street to itself with just a single stop near St James's Palace. Both roads contain a number of art galleries – we take a quick glimpse at each as the bus passes to determine if a little window shopping is in order on the way back should any interesting works be on display.

We turn left into Piccadilly and pass The Wolseley restaurant and The Ritz hotel before stopping at Green Park station. This is an important interchange for road and rail and our loading slightly increases after some alight and more board. The upper-deck is typically just over the half-full mark – who is going to move their bag first to enable another to sit alongside?

The early-morning exercise classes are in full flow in Green Park as we head towards Hyde Park Corner. The Piccadilly junction is one of two arms without traffic signals (Grosvenor Crescent is the other); we may be fortunate and join the circulating throng with minimum delay or instead sit for ages waiting for a gap.

Occasionally our driver's patience wears thin and we pull out regardless – gap or no gap...

Circulating Hyde Park Corner can be an interesting experience if too many (our bus included) have made an inappropriate lane choice; this combined with three sets of traffic signals may thwart our progress, although sometimes it can be greens all the way.

The Hyde Park Corner station bus stop offers more interchange between road and rail – we share stops and exchange passengers with Sloane Street and Brompton Road bus routes. It is also close to The Wellesley hotel which retains the Leslie Green-designed façade of Hyde Park Corner's original station building as its main entrance. We soon pass H R Owen's Ferrari dealership and Harvey Nichols on our nearside and McLaren's showroom – complete with wall-mounted Formula 1 racer – on the offside before making our Knightsbridge stop. A number alight and head towards Brompton Road and its retail premises – Harrods included.

We now have a relatively clear run alongside the Household Cavalry Barracks, Hyde Park and a number of foreign embassies before setting down one or two regulars at Exhibition Road. The Household Cavalry may be out around here exercising their steeds while Shackleton and Scott maintain their vigils on the outside of the

ABOVE: *Golden Tours' sightseeing buses regularly make their garage journeys through Kensington. Volvo 119 (BU14 EHO), a 2014 MCV-bodied B9TL, is not yet sign-written beyond the application of a Gray Line logo (Golden Tours is a franchisee) when seen in Kensington High Street on 21 May 2015.*

ABOVE: *The 328 received an allocation of Wright Gemini Eclipse 3-bodied Volvo B5LH hybrids in 2016. Tower Transit VH38119 (BU16 UXG) heads to the World's End on 21 July 2016.*

Royal Geographical Society's headquarters.

The Royal Albert Hall and Albert Memorial are left behind as we reach Kensington's High Street and set down a number – the bus is much emptier now. Others are dropped off as we proceed to the Addison Road and Holland Road junctions. The latter features the Bristol Cars showroom on its corner (does anything warrant a closer look at lunchtime?) and we are soon crossing the West London Extension Railway line by means of Addison Bridge – hopefully there will be a train in view, either in Kensington Olympia station - located on our offside - or on the lines to the bridge's south.

We pass the Olympia halls and it is time to think about alighting. Access to the North End Road bus stop is usually made difficult by a Tesco lorry unloading in the bus lane – our bus has to use the main traffic lane to get around the obstruction which slows our passage.

Once across North End Road we depress the bell push, gather our baggage and make our way down either staircase. Use the rear staircase too early and we will be shepherded into the lower saloon to prevent us falling from the open platform – try explaining to the platform assistant you co-own a 1951 AEC Regent III with a large opening in its nearside rear corner and know full well how to hold on tight...

We alight at the Brook Green stop remembering to thank our driver as we alight and acknowledge the platform assistant as the bus accelerates towards its next stop – just two to go before terminating at Hammersmith bus station.

The evening return

The evening return is more flexible with choice dictated by time, weather and known road and/or rail problems. The favoured option until July 2014 was a walk to the western end of Kensington High Street before boarding a Routemaster on the heritage variant of route 9 – usually the last one of the day upon which I could bag a front seat upstairs. The crews were without exception most friendly and welcoming; it was a great shame these workings ceased.

On numerous occasions I would board a 9 at Brook Green and alight at Knightsbridge owing to road congestion there or at Hyde Park Corner. A walk through Belgravia to Victoria followed; South Eastern trains run half-hourly from the latter to Eltham – currently extended beyond the evening peak during the rebuilding of London Bridge station. It was also possible to walk from St James's Palace to Charing Cross quicker than the bus when Trafalgar Square was at a standstill – crewed New Routemaster operation made it relatively easy to jump ship from the rear platform when stationary.

And if the weather was conducive to bus photography, I would walk from the office to Victoria or Charing Cross (and in the opposite direction too when the Underground was affected by industrial inaction). The pictures illustrating this feature are a small part of the 3,000-plus accumulated over five years on the 9's route alone.

Sharing

The 9 shares various parts of its route between Charing Cross and Brook Green with 31 other TfL bus services (excluding those that cross its path) plus Green Line route 702 – and its 700 and 701 peak-hour variants. It also shares road space with the many sightseeing tour routes, buses from every tour operator may be seen at different points on route. Particularly evident along the 9's route are the garage journeys made by Golden Tours and City Tour London at both ends of the working day.

Express coaches from further afield may also be seen; National Express, Megabus and Terravision in particular – the first two often diverting from an overly busy A4. Tour coaches are regularly spotted, especially if there is a concert or other event at the Royal Albert Hall or a public exhibition or show at Olympia.

The Hammersmith road served me well during my time working in London. I last used the 9 in August 2016 since when it has lost its platform assistants; the New Routemasters now work solely as driver-operated buses with the rear door closed between stops. That has to be considered a retrograde step and a great shame given that crew operation worked well; the platform assistant often doubling as a guide for any uncertain visitors and being someone to talk with when riding on the rear seats downstairs.

ABOVE: *A busy A4 has probably required this National Express coach to divert via Kensington High Street. Yellow Buses of Bournemouth VCL339 (FJ12 FXT), a 2012 Caetano Levante-bodied Volvo B9R, is seen on 25 September 2015.*

SNAPSHOT
LEICESTER

With a few hours to spare in Leicester on a sunny August day in 2016
Stewart J Brown was impressed by the city's buses.

ABOVE: *Modern double-deckers feature prominently on the streets of Leicester. Those in the Arriva Midlands fleet include ADL Enviro400 MMCs, from a batch of 35 delivered in the summer of 2016. They are 73-seaters. 4508 (YX16 OJH) in Charles Street has route branding for the 84/85 services between Leicester and Lutterworth and South Wigston.*
LEFT: *The newest double-deckers in the First Leicester fleet were 25 Wrightbus StreetDeck integrals, delivered in the spring of 2016. One of these striking buses carries discreet branding for service 54, with the route number above the driver's side window and the legend "up to every 10 mins" above the first upper deck side window. The Leicester StreetDecks are 73-seaters.*
RIGHT: *Among Arriva's single-deckers are six Wrightbus StreetLite DF models which are allocated to service 158 which runs between Leicester and Nuneaton, although 3316 (FJ64 EUD) shows that route branding doesn't always work, as it unloads in Gravel Street outside St Margaret's Bus Station while working on route 27 from Coalville, 12 miles to the north west. Nuneaton is 20 miles to the south west of the city.*

ABOVE: *First also runs StreetLite DF models in Leicester. 63105 (SM13 NCF) is a 41-seater which was new in 2013 to First Manchester. It is loading outside the Haymarket shopping centre.*
BELOW: *There are also older Wrightbus double-deckers in the First Leicester fleet, but on Volvo rather than VDL chassis. 32646 (KP54 AZL) is a 76-seat B7TL dating from 2005 and attractively finished in the livery used by Leicester City Transport in the 1960s, complete with LCT-style fleet number 46.*

ABOVE: *First Leicester 66970 (KX05 MJV), a 2005 Volvo B7RLE with 43-seat Wrightbus Eclipse body., turns from Humberstone Gate in to Charles Street to start a 24-minute round trip on the Highfields Circular.*

RIGHT: *Representative of Arriva's older double-deckers is 4768 (FJ06 ZRN) a 2006 VDL DB250 with Wrightbus Pulsar Gemini 73-seat bodywork.*

BELOW: *While First and Arriva are the main operators in the city, they are not the only ones. Kinchbus operates from Loughborough with a fleet of dedicated Mercedes-Benz Citaros. 905 (BN09 FWY) dates from 2009 and is arriving in the city by way of Belgrave Gate.*

GOING THEIR OWN WAY

SCOTLAND'S BUSES DISCOVERED

All photographs by the author.

ABOVE: ***Eastern Scottish had a strong western Scottish presence in Glasgow, where these two Alexander-bodied Leyland Olympians are seen in May 1985. The lead vehicle is setting out on a 45-mile trip to Edinburgh via Bathgate.***

Celebrating forty years of bus photography, **Peter Rowlands** looks back on his early exposure to the Scottish bus scene, and marvels at the surprises it had in store.

t was like a dream. Buses with gold-leaf fleetnumbers. Bus liveries with heavy black coach lining. Regional bus companies that still had their own separate identities, fleetnames and colour schemes. And lots of front-engined half-cab buses in an era when, outside London, they had almost disappeared.

This was Glasgow in the late 1970s, and to an enthusiast arriving from London it was little short of astounding. Scotland seemed to offer a kind of alternative reality where priorities were different, and where a sense of tradition seemed far stronger than anywhere south of the border.

Probably the buses of the Scottish Bus Group were the biggest surprise. This organisation was the Scottish equivalent of the state-owned National Bus Company in England and Wales,

ABOVE: ***Central SMT ran a number of the comparatively rare short forward-entrance FSF-series Lodekka. They seated 60, ten fewer than the more common FLF.***

LEFT: *Still in service with Midland Scottish in the late 1970s were a number of Alexander-bodied Albion Lowlanders.*

BELOW: *The Greater Glasgow PTE adopted a bright yellow, green and white version of the traditional Glasgow livery. Metrobuses with MCW and Alexander bodywork featured in the fleet. This was the first.*

ABOVE: *The final version of Glasgow's yellow and green livery replaced the white relief with more subtle black. This PTE Ailsa is seen in King's Park.*

and for years NBC had used just two main liveries, red or green, for nearly all its many fleets, applied in unadventurous and uniform fashion, with fleetnames in a common style.

None of that here. Western SMT (maroon), Midland (blue), Central (lighter maroon) all had their own identities and colour schemes, with nothing to convey that they were in common ownership. And when I explored Scotland further, I found that the other SBG fleets followed the same pattern. There was Eastern Scottish's deep green, Fife's vibrant red, Northern's stunning yellow and Highland's vivid red, grey and blue.

Probably Western SMT's deep, gold-leaf fleetname amazed me the most – its slightly antique, blocky upper-case characters, its white highlights, its solid, emphatic underlining. Amazingly, it evoked America's wild west, perhaps implying a bold sense of humour on the part of its designer. A jaunty, cursive version on single-deckers made the same point in a different way.

And then there were the buses themselves – offering a mix subtly different from that found in England. It was no surprise, of course, to see so many double-deckers bodied by Walter Alexander of Falkirk, the local builder, but the

ABOVE: *A PTE Alexander-bodied Leyland Atlantean in all-over Strathclyde orange in George Square, Glasgow, in June 1984.*
BELOW: *Northern Counties was a regular supplier to SBG companies. This Leyland Fleetline of Western SMT is seen crossing the River Clyde on Glasgow Bridge in June 1984.*

ABOVE: *Long before the present-day McGill's tried ex-London articulated buses, the original company put this Leyland-DAB into service on its high-profile Barrhead to Glasgow service. It was previously operated by South Yorkshire PTE.*

ABOVE: *The beginning of the end of the traditional era – the yellow and red of Clydeside Scottish's pre-privatisation livery looks smart on this Dennis Dominator in Greenock in October 1985.*

ABOVE: *The Leyland National was an unfamiliar type in Scotland. This example was operated by AA Motor Services member Youngs, and is seen in Irvine in October 1985.*

ABOVE: *Two unusual Ailsas with bodies built in Ireland by Van Hool-McArdle were operated by A1 Service member Tom Hunter. This one, which has been preserved, is heading through Ardrossan on its way to Kilmarnock in October 1985.*

ubiquity of the company's Y-type single-deckers seemed extraordinary. They were everywhere. Leylands, AECs, Fords, Bedfords, Albions, Seddons – whatever the chassis, it seemed Alexander had a Y-type bus body for it: and if you didn't like the high floor on all these models, too bad.

What was missing, it gradually dawned on me, were Leyland National and Bristol RE single-deckers, which proved great rarities. In place of the rattle of the National's Leyland 500 engine, so common in English cities, Glasgow's streets resounded with roar of the Leopard.

In fact the only REs I ever saw in Scotland featured Alexander's striking M-type coach bodywork, with its slanting window pillars and embossed side stripes – further examples of American influence on Scotland's bus scene. Sadly, I arrived too late to photograph these remarkable coaches in their original black and white livery (Western SMT) or black and yellow (Eastern Scottish); by the time I arrived, they all seemed to be white and blue.

On the double-deck front, I was struck by the large number of surviving front-engined Bristol Lodekkas in the SBG fleets, including rarities (to me, anyway) such as short-wheelbase front-entrance FSF examples in the Central fleet. And there were still some ancient-looking blue

ABOVE: *ECW became a major body supplier to Lothian Region Transport in the early 1980s. This long-wheelbase Leyland Olympian is turning into Princes Street, Edinburgh, in October 1985*

Albion Lowlanders in the Midland fleet – again a type I had never encountered in England.

Another surprise was the number of double-deck bodies by Northern Counties, especially in SBG fleets. In similar NBC companies south of the border the make was relatively uncommon. Alexander didn't have the market entirely to itself.

Among modern buses, Volvo Ailsas were particularly noticeable, especially when I ventured further afield. But was it a little retrospective to adopt a bus that looked as if it had a rear-mounted engine, when actually it was at the front?

Perhaps, because an apparently a similar yearning for the tried and tested seemed to have prompted SBG to encourage the development of Seddon's Pennine VII single-deck underfloor-engined range – Leopard lookalikes with established and reliable Gardner engines. With their familiar Y-type bodies, they seemed like Leopards by another name.

When Seddon disappeared from the bus market in the early 1980s, Dennis stepped into the breach with its Dorchester, and yet again SBG was an eager customer. Intriguingly, by this point Alexander had developed its TC coach-style body, which at a glance looked somewhat reminiscent of the equivalent from Plaxtons.

There were other locally-inspired developments too – for instance, MCW Metrobuses with Alexander bodywork, which seemed a great curiosity. The first three even had what looked like a variation of the old AL body with its peaked front dome.

There were local authority bus operators as well as SBG fleets, of course – though here again, Alexander bodywork dominated, especially in Glasgow. In 1977 Greater Glasgow Passenger Transport Executive's livery was a rather bright version of the city's traditional orange/yellow and green, with extensive use of white relief; and Greater Glasgow had adopted the rather non-specific "Trans-Clyde" as its fleetname. When I returned a few years later the white had been dropped, and to my mind the result was if anything more elegant. Tradition was still alive.

In Edinburgh, I never saw the long-standing mid-green of SBG's Scottish Omnibuses, long known as SOL. By the late 1970s the company was trading as Eastern Scottish, and had adopted a darker green livery. I heard that die-hards disliked it, though for me it evoked fond memories of the much-lamented Tilling green, abandoned many years before by NBC.

What impressed me about Edinburgh's council-owned fleet was the persistence of the elegant

ABOVE: *Tayside Regional Transport bought a batch of Alexander-bodied Bristol VRTs in the mid-1970s. This one still looked smart in summer 1980, but by the following year it had been sold to Western Welsh, and later worked for its successor Red & White.*

ABOVE: *Leyland Atlanteans and Daimler Fleetlines with visually similar Alexander bodywork typified the Grampian fleet when this shot of a 1978 Atlantean was taken in October 1985.*

mainly-maroon livery (or madder, as I learned to call it). I was also intrigued a few years later to find so many Eastern Coachworks bodies here, looking particularly striking on the long-wheelbase Leyland Olympians that gradually dominated the fleet.

Up in Dundee, I more or less missed the drab green livery of the municipal fleet, by this time run by Tayside Regional Council, but was greatly impressed by the vibrant two-tone blue livery that had replaced it. And here was a great curiosity – Bristol VR double-deckers with peaked Alexander bodywork: a rare combination. What I didn't know was that Dundee would decide these were unreliable, and sell them off within just a few years.

Dundee was very much home to the Volvo Ailsa, of which Tayside bought more than 160 examples. And here was another surprise – Ailsas with bodywork by East Lancashire Coachbuilders alongside the more numerous Alexander-bodied examples.

Aberdeen (strictly speaking Grampian Regional Council) still used a relatively traditional-looking livery for its fleet – cream and green with an orange relief band when I first went there. Both Daimler

*ABOVE: **Classic Midland livery, classic shot in Perth: an Alexander-bodied Daimler Fleetline in August 1984. Among all SBG companies, the blue corporate fleetname unsurprisingly worked best in this fleet.***

*ABOVE: **The elegance of the Midland Scottish blue was replaced in the Strathtay fleet by a garishly mismatched blue and orange, as seen on this Alexander-bodied Ailsa in Perth in October 1985.***

ABOVE: *Lowering skies hover over these two similar-looking Alexander-bodied Highland buses in Inverness bus station – a Ford of 1974 and a much older AEC Reliance dating from 1966. They are in Farraline Park bus station in August 1980.*

Fleetlines and Leyland Atlanteans were to be found here, and to my untutored eye their peaked Alexander bodies seemed virtually indistinguishable from one another. More striking to my mind were the intensely yellow buses of Northern, still sporting their own style of fleetname on my fist visit.

Inverness proved another eye-opener. SBG subsidiary Highland Omnibuses' livery of red and grey was topped off by a vivid green-blue colour known as peacock blue, and buses still carried an elaborate circular emblem featuring a golden eagle. The effect was stunning, and the turnout seemed universally immaculate.

In both Northern and Highland fleets, bodywork by ECW, albeit on Fleetlines, not Bristol VRs, made a welcome change from the ubiquity of Alexander bodywork.

Another striking discovery in Scotland was the existence of so many substantial independent companies. In Paisley, for example, Graham's Bus Service seemed almost like an alternative municipal company, while in Wishaw Hutchisons played a similar role. Meanwhile, in Ayr and Ardrossan two independent cooperatives held sway – AA Motor Services and A1 Service respectively.

It couldn't last. I kept coming back to Scotland, but the strongly traditional flavour of my first visit was steadily diluted. First, Scottish Bus Group adopted a standard fleetname style for all its companies. That seemed a shame in itself, but worse was the fact that it was always blue, rather than colours that might have complemented the individual liveries.

However, at least those liveries survived for a few years longer. But then more changes followed as the SBG companies were subdivided and prepared for privatisation. The newly invented Clydeside Scottish's red and yellow livery seemed to work pretty effectively, but others were more questionable; the orange and blue of Strathtay in Perth struck me as a particularly violent colour clash.

Meanwhile, Strathclyde PTE (the new entity running Glasgow's public transport) finally abandoned the long-standing yellow and green livery in favour of a relentlessly uniform all-over orange, broken only by matt black along the skirt and around the lower deck windows.

In the end, all this would be swept away. Privatisation loomed, and with it would come a total change in almost every large bus fleet in Scotland (except for Edinburgh's).

But that's another story.

MERSEYSIDE MEMORIES

John Robinson looks back at the buses of the Merseyside PTE.

ABOVE: *Liverpool Corporation was one of the few operators of unpainted buses, a number of AEC Regents and Leyland Titans appearing in this form, albeit with green relief. Ten of a batch of 30 Leyland PD2s were finished with unpainted anodised aluminium panels as an experiment to save on repainting costs; they were referred to by staff as Silver Bullets. Built in 1957 with Crossley body frames, it was intended that the coachwork would be completed by the Corporation at its Edge Lane works. However, due to an unforeseen vehicle surplus, all 30 (L280-L309) were held in store there until being sent to Metro-Cammell to complete the bodywork, finally entering service in 1961 as Liverpool's last front-engined buses. They retained their pre-booked registration numbers (VKB 736-765) which had been issued in May 1956 even though, by 1961, Liverpool was issuing reversed registrations. New to Green Lane depot, by the early 1970s many of the batch moved to Litherland for operation on the 28 and the 50 group services which were operated jointly with Ribble. L303 (VKB 759) turns out of Islington into Commutation Row on 17 November 1973 on service 58 from Litherland to Old Haymarket. This was the last unpainted bus to remain in service, being withdrawn in December 1975.*

The Merseyside Passenger Transport Executive commenced operations on 1 December 1969 when the municipal transport undertakings of Liverpool, Birkenhead and Wallasey were merged. From this date the PTE assumed responsibility for a fleet of around 1,300 buses and several ferries, at this time the only maritime interests of any PTE. Subsequent boundary changes and local government reorganisation brought the St Helens and Southport undertakings into the PTE on 1 April 1974, adding a further 200 buses to the fleet.

Initially, the PTE split its operations into three divisions; the former Birkenhead and Wallasey operations, including the Mersey ferries, became the responsibility of the Wirral Division whilst Liverpool was split into two divisions, North and South. With the later addition of Southport and St Helens these two operations became Districts within the existing, although from then enlarged, North and South Divisions respectively.

RIGHT: *Liverpool was one of the first operators to place a major order for the Leyland Atlantean, 200 being delivered between November 1962 and September 1964 (L500-L699). Their Metro-Cammell bodywork was to a Liverpool design and incorporated styling features that were influenced by contemporary car design and was visually a great improvement on the bodybuilder's standard rear-engine body of the time. On the first 60 buses the rear cutaway, above the engine compartment, extended half way up the upper-deck rear end (as in this view) but this feature wasn't liked by the operator so subsequent buses had standard height cutaways. Prince Alfred Road-based L548 (548 KD), operating service 73B to Childwall Park Avenue, stands in Georges Dock Way, Liverpool, on 17 November 1973 outside the Art Deco Georges Dock Building, which was the head office of the Mersey Tunnels and included within its structure a tall ventilation shaft for the first Mersey Tunnel (Queensway) which opened in 1934. A further 180 broadly similar buses entered service between 1965 and 1967 (L700-L879).*

Of the four original PTEs, Merseyside was the only one to adopt two different liveries. North and South Divisions retained the former Liverpool livery of green and cream; Wirral Division, however, began to use blue and cream, or off-white, from April 1970, changing to a darker shade of blue, and pale lemon, in February 1972. The red and cream liveries of St Helens and Southport were retained for a few months following takeover.

With the expansion of the PTE, and the need to present a corporate identity, a new livery of Verona green and Jonquil cream was introduced for the whole fleet in October 1974. Towards the end of the 1970s dark brown skirts and window surrounds began to be added to this livery. The Southport District open-top fleet retained the municipal red and cream, there being strong opposition in the resort to the loss of this livery.

This selection of pictures, taken between 1973 and1984, illustrates the diversity of the fleet and its operating area.

ABOVE: *In the mid 1970s the bus building industry was unable to keep up with the high levels of demand for new vehicles which led to several of the L500-L699 Atlanteans, withdrawal of which had commenced in 1975, being overhauled at Edge Lane works and returned to service. These buses were completely re-trimmed internally and lost their detachable ribbed aluminium skirt panels, designed to contain minor accident damage to the lower area of the body, in favour of painted aluminium panels. Typifying this is 533 (533 KD), one of four transferred to Laird Street, Birkenhead, to assist with the depot's conversion to one-man-operation, replacing former Birkenhead Corporation Leyland Titans, which may well have been younger than the Atlanteans. Since Wirral Division buses didn't have fleet numbers with prefixes, the 'L' was omitted from the fleet number on these Atlanteans so former L533 became 533. As well as painting over the 'L' on the fleet number plates, the number was also repeated on the front and sides as seen in this view at Laird Street on 20 July 1979. Standard MPTE Alexander-bodied Leyland Atlantean 1365 (DKC 365L), new to Wirral Division in 1973, stands alongside.*

ABOVE: *St Helens Corporation was the only constituent operator of MPTE not to operate rear-engined double-deckers, purchasing AEC Regents and Leyland Titans as late as 1967; from the following year it only bought single-deckers in the form of AEC Swifts. 54 (MDJ 554E), from the final batch of four Leyland Titan PD2A/27s with East Lancs bodywork, is depicted at Warrington Arpley bus station on 24 September 1979 on service 329 to Rainford which was, at the time, operated jointly with Ribble and Crosville. It is fitted with the fibreglass St Helens bonnet, introduced in 1960, so-named because it had been developed jointly by St Helens Corporation and Leyland. This type of bonnet, with its sculpted front corner, gave the driver a much less restricted kerb-side view than Leyland's earlier design of enclosed radiator.*

ABOVE: *In 1968-69 Liverpool Corporation took delivery of 110 Leyland Panthers with Metro-Cammell bodies seating 47, with space for 24 standing passengers (1001-1110), in order to introduce wide-scale omo, at the time the largest programme of its type outside London. They were painted in a mainly cream livery with green window surrounds, intended to signify the need to pay fares to the driver; however, from 1971 the vast majority were repainted in reversed green and cream livery. Green Lane depot's 1092 (RKA 971G) still retained its original colours when photographed turning out of Islington into Commutation Row on 17 November 1973 operating service 17D from Fazakerley to Pier Head, one of the early routes to be converted to omo. The Panthers introduced a new four-digit fleet numbering system (1001 onwards being for Leylands) whereby the letter prefix indicating chassis manufacturer was dropped; they also introduced fleet number plates which were retrofitted to the Atlanteans but none of the older buses. Another 25 omo single-deckers were purchased by Liverpool in the form of Park Royal-bodied Bristol REs. Although double-deck omo had been permissible since 1966, the uptake by operators was generally slow as the future, in large cities in particular, was considered to be single-deck operation, and it took another three years before it was introduced in Merseyside*

ABOVE: *The series from 2001 upwards was used for Bristols. Ordered by Liverpool, but delivered to MPTE in 1970, 2026 (UKD 520J) was the first of 24 dual-doorway 33ft-long East Lancs-bodied Bristol VRTs (2026-2049) specifically built for omo; a twenty-fifth chassis, which was to have become 2027, was destroyed in the fire at East Lancs in March 1970, and so the remaining vehicles became 2027-2049 and the number 2050 was not used. A further 35 similar vehicles, also ordered by Liverpool, entered service in 1971 (2051-2085). Like the Liverpool Atlanteans, all these VRTs originally had ribbed aluminium skirts but most vehicles had these changed, upon overhaul, to painted aluminium panels. In this form, and wearing Verona green and Jonquil cream livery with brown skirt and window surrounds, 2026 was one of the last four survivors of the 'Jumbo' VRTs and is depicted in Ormskirk Road, Aintree, picking up spectators after the Grand National on 9 April 1983.*

ABOVE: *MPTE was an early customer for the Metro-Scania, an integrally-built design by Metro-Cammell Weymann with Scania running units, with 20 entering service in 1972 numbered 4001-20. The first eight were allocated to Wirral Division and were painted in that Division's blue and lemon livery whilst the remainder entered service in Liverpool painted green and cream. Liverpool-based 4009 (CKD 409L) is depicted on 8 August 1978 in the lofty surroundings of Edge Lane Works, opened by Liverpool Corporation in 1928. Directly behind, also in Liverpool green, is 4024 (PKD 424M) one of sixty Metropolitans (the Metro-Scania's double-decker equivalent) which entered the fleet in 1974-75, divided between Liverpool's Green Lane and Prince Alfred Road depots.*

ABOVE: *The last double-deckers delivered to Southport Corporation prior to its absorption into the PTE were ten Leyland Atlanteans with Alexander AL-type bodywork (81-90). Although to the casual observer they may have appeared similar to the PTE's existing Alexander-bodied Atlanteans, they did in fact have several differences, the main ones being the dual-doorways, engine shrouds, front dash panel, window rubbers and the upper-deck front window design with a slender metal pillar dividing the two panes of glass, mirroring that of the windscreen. However, following accident damage, 84 (VWM 84L) received a modified Alexander upper-deck front, and destination indicators, of the type already used by the PTE, with the window pillar incorporated within the fibreglass molding. It is depicted heading south along Lord Street on service 3 to Guildford Road on 9 April 1977. As a concession to the former Southport livery of red and cream, in the early days red wheel hubs were retained on some buses when repainted into MPTE livery although this practice later ceased. In addition, on the Atlanteans, the Verona green was initially extended below the upper saloon waistline to include the area where the upper red band previously was although on this modified bus this feature isn't present.*

ABOVE: *Two Leyland 550FG truck chassis with Alexander (Belfast) 22-seat bus bodies (331/2) were delivered to Wirral Division in 1974 to operate a shoppers' service inherited from Wallasey, to replace a 19-seat Redford J2 new to Wallasey in 1967. Delivered in Wirral Division's blue and lemon livery, they were repainted in Verona green with Jonquil cream window surrounds prior to entering service, subsequently receiving the later version with more cream as seen on 332 (RKA 424N), by now with dark brown window surrounds, at the former Wallasey Corporation Seaview Road, Liscard, depot on 1 April 1983. They were very unreliable and often had to be replaced by a Metro-Scania or Leyland National which prevented the whole route being covered as the FGs were the only buses that could get round some of the roads that the route traversed.*

ABOVE: *Leyland Atlanteans were the most numerous type in the MPTE fleet, with Alexander becoming the main bodywork supplier, although East Lancs, Metro-Cammell and Willowbrook bodywork also featured. Typifying Alexander's AL-type bodywork, which was purchased from 1972 to 1984, is Speke depot's 1604 (GKA 29N), dating from 1974, in Park Place, Toxteth, on 10 October 1984, operating service 82C from Pier Head to Speke.*

ABOVE: *St Helens Corporation took delivery of 63 Marshall-bodied AEC Swifts between 1968 and 1973 whilst a further nine which were on order were delivered to the PTE in 1975. These were easily recognisable by their former Bootle (EM) registration numbers rather than the traditional St Helens registration (DJ). 284 (GEM 604N) heads along Baldwin Street in St Helens town center on 21 June 1984 and shows the brighter single-deck livery used from 1977 whereby the Verona green was restricted to the skirt and roof.*

ABOVE: *MPTE purchased a number of small batches of vehicles for evaluation purposes between 1979 and 1984 which were numbered in an 00xx series. Amongst these were 15 MCW Metrobuses split over two batches. The first five, delivered in 1979-80, were complete MCW products (the first two with Gardner engines and the others powered by Rolls Royce) but the second batch carried Alexander R-type bodywork. From the first batch, Rolls Royce-powered 0022 (UKA 22V), new in 1980, heads along Lord Street, Liverpool, on service 14C from Croxteth to Pier Head, operated by Gillmoss depot, on 1 April 1983.*

ABOVE: *Although eight Leyland Nationals, dating from 1974, were acquired with the Southport Corporation fleet, the PTE did not obtain any further Nationals until 1977-78 when 30 entered service. The following year another 34 arrived (6001-6034). Green Lane-based 6004 (SKF 4T) stands at Pier Head bus station on 20 July 1979 operating service 17C to Fazakerley.*

ABOVE: *Although ex-London Transport DMS Daimler Fleetlines were popular with operators the length and breadth of the country, including with some PTEs, none were purchased by MPTE. However, former DMS321 (JGF 321K), with Park Royal bodywork, became a demonstrator for Brockhouse Maxwell transmissions and was on loan to the PTE at St Helens where it received temporary fleet number 8000. It is depicted in Broad Lane, Collins Green, approaching the bridge over the original Liverpool and Manchester Railway at Collins Green, operating service 329 from Warrington to Rainford, on 2 August 1984.*

ABOVE: *Two batches of Volvo Ailsa B55s with Alexander RV-type bodies were placed in service in Wirral Division, two in 1982 and 13 in 1984. From the second batch 0078 (A160 HLV) stands at Birkenhead's Woodside bus station on 10 October 1984 operating the Oxton Circle service 91, which was the first omo double-deck service in Merseyside when introduced by Birkenhead Corporation in October 1969; a week later omo double-deck operation commenced in Liverpool.*

ABOVE: *The final Liverpool half-cab buses comprised both AEC Regents and Leyland Titans, with the last being withdrawn in 1976. Presenting a sombre sight at Tommy Goodwin's scrapyard in Boulder Bridge Lane, Carlton, Barnsley on 23 July 1975, is 1957 Metro-Cammell-bodied AEC Regent V A192 (VKB 790) which had been withdrawn the year before from Prince Alfred Road depot. It is quite possible that its 77A destination, a works service between the city and the Dunlop tyre factory at Speke, is indicative of its final service journey.*

BUS BLUES

Robert E Jowitt visits Oxford and Cambridge in attempt to find up-to-date if old-fashioned real printed information on timetables.

ABOVE: *A fine example of the almost unrecognisable up-dated colours of Stagecoach approaching Carfax from The High, Oxford, in April 2017 backed by ebullient Victorian/Edwardian banking baroque.*

My premise in writing these words is that when I was young half a century ago and even later when I was not so young it was usually pretty easy almost anywhere to obtain a proper printed timetable of local transport services; and that in this present era this is largely no longer easy and sometimes even impossible. You are told it is all available on the internet or some such devilish device, such as I use rarely, unwillingly, and with some loathing. In such circumstance I have tried of late to discover what may be available to the Luddite, and more particularly in the great University cities, dark and light blue, of Oxford and Cambridge, such, we are told, being the colours of the beefy teams rowing the Thames in the Oxford and Cambridge Boat Race.

No sane person save in most dire case would attempt to drive a motorcar into these places; it is far better to use either the park-and-ride facilities from the peripheries or to arrive by train at the railway stations. Both are also readily accessible by motor coach, with usefully central termini.

I think I had visited Cambridge only once, in 1965, before my daughter took up residence there in recent years, while the Railway Photographic Circle, which I was invited to join, held its meetings there or abouts. Oxford I had known on and off much longer.

In the light blue case, with forays of increasing frequency, it behoved me to discover more on the local bus services. In the beginning there were bus stops immediately outside the station, with services to take you to the city centre for change to anywhere else. The stop signs told you most of what you wanted to know. Recently these stops were moved a tedious distance from the station's mouth to cope with the guided busway, four different stops, certainly passably-well informed, but by the time you had seen a bus arrive at the furthest stop and worked out it might be for you it had moved on. The station information racks offered nothing at all on adjacent bus services. If you came from some far-away country you might well wonder how to proceed hence; I did anyway.

I think that my first visit at this period was by car with a friend, in which, as part of a windmill hunt, we looked at the incipient but far from complete bus-way, and then betook ourselves to park and ride. We were rather pleased with ourselves that we managed to photograph three p&rs together in the various red, blue and green liveries. On return to the car-park I grabbed from the waiting room a leaflet, the only edition of leaflet present, in hopes it was a chart of p&r services. It proved to be a questionnaire on 'How was your journey?'. I duly sent it in with complaint of the absence of more information on park-and-ride and, incidentally, mentioning that the drivers both in and out appeared to have viewed my OAP travel-card askance, as if they deemed me scrounging.

I must say that very soon I received a reply from Stagecoach supplying details of p&r and a promise that they were educating their staff in customer relations. To be fair I may add that since then

ABOVE: *A study in diminishing buses. This roaring Oxford scene is just outside Gloucester Green coach station.*

ABOVE: *Rival traction to the fore in Oxford. Stagecoach Gold is so impressive a change from previous liveries and vehicle specifications as to be almost unidentifiable to eyes familiar with days of yore. The bus is a Scania N230UD with 73-seat ADL Enviro400 body.*

I have never met quite such gloomy fellows.

I should add, moreover, that any reminiscences that I offer herewith are of diverse particular days and need not be regarded as the normal quotidian situation. I took it as I found it; the next day might have produced entirely different results (or, as in the case of timetables, sometimes nil.) Besides which exuberance in describing delights – or otherwise – of travel may possibly not present an entirely accurate record of verisimilitude.

My daughter, resident in Chesterton, usually cycles to the station to commute to London, but she has a Filofax and a printed timetable of the Chesterton bus, for the city centre stop of which any bus from the station will take you. At this stop we wait half an hour at least, while buses for Chesterton are promised on the display unit and

then wiped off. The unit may be faulty, but even if such is not the fault of Stagecoach, the failure of the promised bus to arrive and the next ditto must surely be attributed to their door. On the other hand the bus, on appearing, does carry proper printed timetables of its services. Hurrah!

This is route 2. Her nearest, five minutes from her door, is the 17, but only every two hours with bus-stop timetables so battered as to be illegible if not absent. It so happened I saw the 17, an Optare, head out to the nearby terminus, so resolved to catch it back to town, knowing it served the spot I sought. The stop chanced to be in the midst of road-works with plentiful cones. The bus approached, I held out my hand, he gesticulated to move onwards, which I did, while he waited.

'Thanks,' I said, and added, 'They should

put out a temporary bus-stop.' 'They don't care!' he replied bitterly.

At the next stop the doors shut themselves across an old lady boarding. 'Sorry,' he said, 'they do that!'

The old lady didn't seem to mind, indeed seemed to recognise both the driver and the bad habits of bus. It behaved little better the rest of the way, other drivers on the pavements at the central stops in truth smirked derisively at it.

My destination was an ale-house entitled the Tram Shed. It is in the correct position for the horse-tram era, though more likely stables than car shed, the latter being adjacent but probably devoid of any originality save a couple of rails. Further rails, in two sets laid with the grooves all on the same side, strain the imagination. It serves, however, a good pint.

Not long after this Stagecoach abandoned the 17 which fell then to Whippet, who cranked it up to hourly but scrapped afternoon working altogether... and chopped it from going as far as the Tram Shed. I suspect this take-over to be political, as the route passes the site of the new Chesterton station (still at the time of writing under construction), where the main Ely railway is joined by the derelict railway of which the further reaches provide the busway to St Ives. This dead length must surely soon become more busway, but my daughter does not know the final pattern, and nor do I.

On the subject of the busway I must relate that some time after finally – following many vicissitudes and delays – it was opened I rode on it in the failing light of a bleak January late Sunday afternoon, out to St Ives. I had a pint in a St Ives pub and caught the next bus back. The passage through the abandoned gravel pits was by no means without artistic merit, and the sight of the windmill on its nearby hill a delight; the rest of the route was not memorable. I found the motion to be a very slightly sea-sick nature. My daughter reports rumours that buses occasionally 'de-rail'. The main defect in the system is, however, that once the buses leave the railway they are plunged into the crawling maelstrom of Cambridge road traffic.

Apart from the Tram Shed other of my researches were directed towards the availability of printed timetables. As I have said, the railway station has none. 'We're not allowed to put them there,' someone in authority told me. The enquiry office at Drummer Street has closed for eternity. A comely plump young lady waiting at a stop saw me peering at a panel and ask if she could help; I replied I was seeking times to Ely, but as I then spotted them adjacent I simply thanked her for her kindness. Thus the only source for timetable leaflets was the tourist information office; 'But they may be out of date,' the lady informed me, over as many (not, I think, all the routes) as she could furnish. So far as an overall route map was concerned the only source offering one was the tourist information in...Ely!

Wondering whether this situation in general might amount to discrimination against the elderly who find internet access difficult or even impossible, and having an opportunity this spring 2017 to catch a park-and-ride into Oxford, I decided to study the dark-blue case.

My last serious experience of buses here had been ten, perhaps twenty years before, or longer, when there had been much discussion on the ill fact that City of Oxford would not accept return tickets from other operators on the same route; and vice versa. I am given to believe this discouraging situation is now resolved to the traveller's satisfaction. At all events the p&r terminus provided a handsome array of leaflets for a considerable number of routes and a good system map.

The City of Oxford bus moreover was of startling modernity, its upper deck including two sets of fore-and-aft seats with dining-car tables and a variation of chaise-longue, this latter almost suitable as a bed for the pose of Manet's infamously provocative unclad young lady entitled Olympia.

At Gloucester Green coach station I was distracted, I must admit, by enquiring about coach services to Brussels, and did not pay as much attention as I should have to local matters in the local enquiry offices there present, save to note a general efficiency and quantity of staff. The only Stagecoach timetable I picked up was indeed snatched later in the day from a Wantage-bound bus halted outside Christchurch.

The tourist information offered more of the same stuff as at the p&r, and, unlike the threat – even if unproven – from Cambridge, up to date!

I have to admit that this visit was of only a few hours duration, and with relations, though entirely tolerant, requiring other diversions than bus offices, such as inspections of college gateways, the enticing covered market and even Oxfam shops.

I could have done with much more time, should have tried to find it.

Never mind, on my return home I spread out a tide of leaflets, and added then those from Cambridge, studied them, and then started on the telephone.

In this view from the main entrance of Cambridge railway station is where the bus-stops used to be but they are now removed somewhat inconveniently further away. A new cycle park and who knows what else are under construction in the autumn of 2015.

A Stagecoach Enviro400 departs from Drummer Street bus station, across the mouth of Emmanuel Street. But in Cambridge many people prefer to cycle

ABOVE: *Admittedly hardly an original composition, but this Mercedes-Benz Citaro of the Oxford Bus Company graphically displays the worthy practice of dedicated buses on its routes in the city.*

Firstly, from an omnibus friend, I learnt that the Oxford urban routes now not only accepted rival tickets but also were jointly operated by City and Stagecoach, even if outer routes were still even viciously rival. This, to my observations from the pavement, had not been readily apparent, but all vehicles seemed so magnificently modern that the difference would require closer study. Time, time!

City of Oxford, responding to my request, sent copious timetables which had not been available on the spot... by return of post. Stagecoach in Cambridge replied with a complete set – up to date – very soon after, while the damsel who answered the phone said I would probably have found them in the p&r termini had I arrived thither. Whippet, for more of the Cambridge area, responded pretty fast too, with a decently comprehensive map with timetables of their field of operation. Stagecoach in Oxford promised at my first call to send straightaway what I required. After many days had elapsed with nothing arriving I tried again. It meant a great many pieces of paper, this maid replied, rather doubtfully, but she would see what could be done. At the deadline for submission of this essay this is nil – not, admittedly, I had told her my intention of writing an article. Would it have made much, any, difference?

To the readers of my dark and light blue adventures the failures in my methods of seeking answers to my enquiries must prove all too obvious. Quite apart from my lack of attention in Gloucester Green, Oxford, I should have visited the Oxford Bus information office elsewhere but at that moment I did not know it existed. Likewise I should have inspected how the railway station might compare with the desert of that in Cambridge. As for more on Cambridge, I should have tried to prove the truth of the damsel's words on what I would discover at p&r termini. Other things left undone may be apparent.

Whatever the truth of these various issues, does it have to be necessary to achieve such lengths to receive such information? Must I telephone every bus company to ascertain essential information? Should enquiry offices be shut down? To be sure they cost money to the companies in times of belt-drawing-in, and when the use of a lot of printed paper could be deemed undesirable or even un-ecological expense? Yet I repeat that the proper printed timetable to be carried in pocket or handbag is not simply an aid to the nearly-senile and computer-illiterate-and-inept – and an unfair prejudice against such persons - but a positive reminder of the presence of the bus in the life of any potential passengers.

To which, of course, amiable drivers and decent vehicles must prove a major enhancement; I have said above that the attitudes in Cambridge appear to have improved, and the latest news - to me at least – is that Stagecoach in Cambridge is indulging (may have already when you read this) in major fleet renewal. I wonder, will they have Pullman dining tables and chaise-longue on the upper deck? To be fair to Stagecoach – which some readers might deem I have not so proved – I must say that on this visit in autumn 2015 (whence date the accompanying photographs) there were certain buses of such startling newness as to render me nearly incapable of realising that such was a Stagecoach new-look, being all too aware of a great quantity of vehicles with only the mildest of modification to the antiquated red blue and orange.

In conclusion I might add, as mentioned already at the commencement of this essay, that motor coach services arrive sensibly fairly near the centres of both cities. Gloucester Green in Oxford has many facilities, Parkside - by Parker's Piece - in Cambridge less so, being so far as I can see a line of mildly inadequate bus-type-shelters under an avenue of albeit handsome but rain-dripping trees.

Now it must be obvious that many persons might desire to travel between the two blue cities, and as any railways towards this purpose have years since been destroyed it is essential, to achieve this aim, to travel by coach. Of a truth there is a coach service achieving just this. Having learnt that this is controlled from Bedford – probably or possibly half-way – I duly telephoned to Bedford to request a printed timetable of the services on offer. I had the impression this was a strange request, and might be answered only with difficulty. I have not so far received a printed timetable in response.

Suppose, just suppose, that I care to revisit either city, or both cities one after the other, to cover and discover more on those failures I have admitted above, how do I ascertain the times for journeying from dark to light blue? Or, verily, light blue to dark? Obviously I must go forth to be on the front line of Gloucester Green or Parkside, to read what is told at the stops.

Forward planning by means of a printed paper timetable is not, so far as I can understand, an option. Is this, I have to ask (albeit hide-bound as I am in traditional practice), is this really progress?

ABOVE: *Typical Jowitt, shooting against the sun, for a non-standard Stagecoach livery, predominantly pink to support a cancer charity. Similar trees to these splatter raindrops on the coach stops along Parkside*